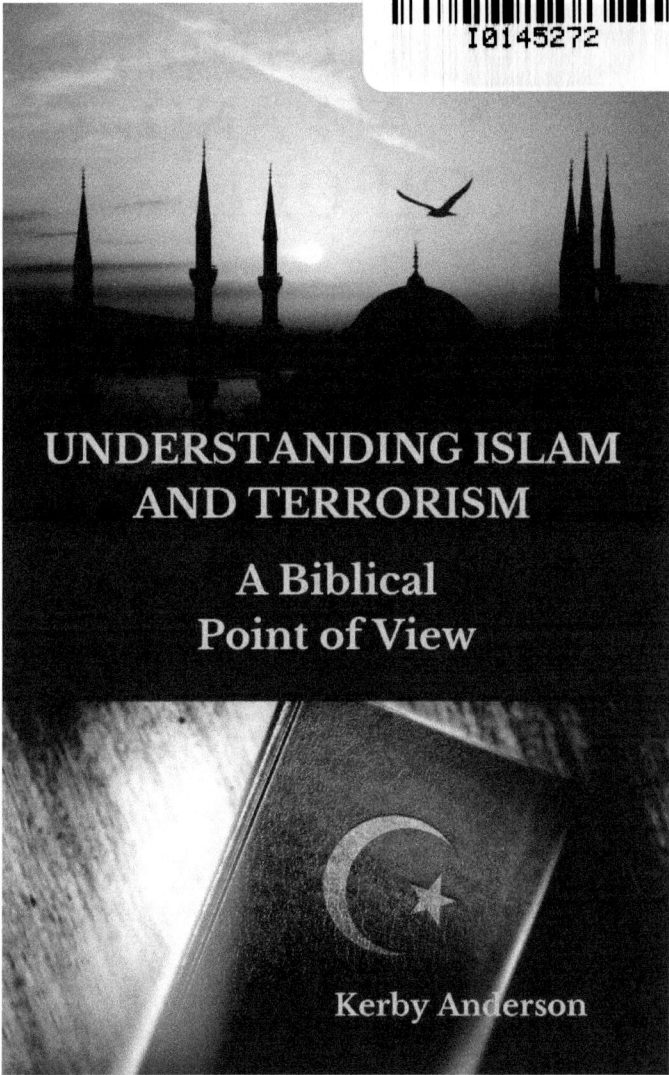

# UNDERSTANDING ISLAM AND TERRORISM

## A Biblical Point of View

Kerby Anderson

# UNDERSTANDING ISLAM AND TERRORISM

# A Biblical Point of View

Kerby Anderson

Christian Publishing House

Cambridge, Ohio

Christian Publishing House
Professional Conservative Christian
Publishing of the Good News!

CPH Since 2005

*UNDERSTANDING ISLAM AND TERRORISM: A Biblical Point of View* by Kerby Anderson

ISBN-13: **978-1-945757-61-7**

ISBN-10: **1-945757-61-2**

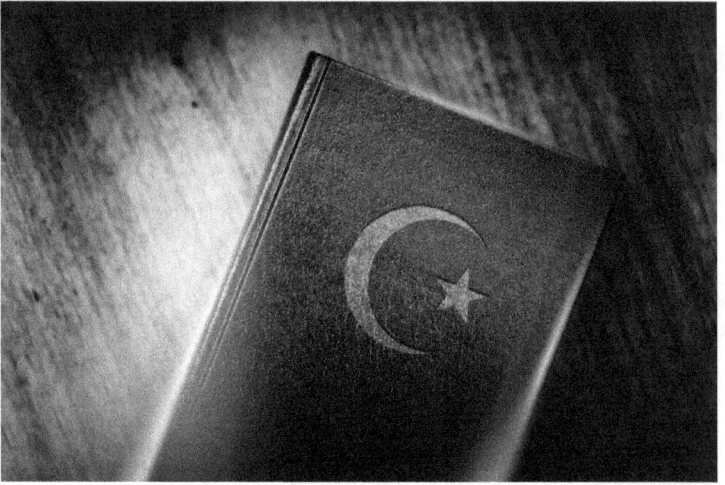

# Table of Contents

## Kerby Anderson

**Kerby Anderson** is the President of Probe Ministries. He holds master's degrees from Yale University (science) and Georgetown University (government).

He also serves as a visiting professor at Dallas Theological Seminary and has spoken on dozens of university campuses including University of Michigan, Vanderbilt University, Princeton University, Johns Hopkins University, University of Colorado and University of Texas.

He is the author of eighteen books including *Signs of Warning, Signs of Hope, Moral Dilemmas, Christian Ethics in Plain Language, A Biblical Point of View on Islam, A Biblical Point of View on Homosexuality, A Biblical Point of View on Intelligent Design, A Biblical Point of View on Spiritual Warfare*, and *Managing Your Money in Tough Times*. He is the author of a new book series: *Christians and Government, Christians and Economics, Technology and Social Trends*, and *Arts, Media, and Culture*.

He is the host of "Point of View" radio talk. He has appeared or numerous radio and TV talk shows including the "MacNeil/Lehrer News Hour," "Focus on the Family," "Beverly LaHaye Live," and "The 700 Club."

He produces a daily syndicated radio commentary and writes editorials that have appeared in the *Dallas Morning News*, the *Miami Herald*, the *San Jose Mercury*, and the *Houston Post*. His radio commentaries have been syndicated by International Media Services, United Press International, American Family Radio, Moody Radio, and the USA Radio Network.

Kerby is married to Susanne and is the father of three grown children.

# INTRODUCTION

Although Islam had been a major world religion that began 1400 years ago, most people only began to pay attention to it after September 11, 2001, when terrorists struck America. In the sixteen years following we have seen horrific attacks in Barcelona, Beslan, Boston, Brussels, London, Madrid, Mumbai, Nice, Orlando, Paris, and San Bernardino. Some were large-scale coordinated attacks. Others were perpetrated by what experts called a "lone wolf." Of course, we can also add to this kidnapping and beheadings of journalists, tourists, and committed Christians.

As someone who regularly speaks and conducts radio interviews on Islam and terrorism, I wanted to put together a book that answers many of the questions that surface in speeches and broadcasts. Why do radical Muslims hate us? Why do these Islamists hate Western civilization? What do Muslims believe? How can I witness to my Muslim friends, neighbors, and coworkers?

The need for clear thinking has never been greater. Political correctness and multiculturalism dominate the thinking in both media and the academy. Anyone who dares to evaluate Islam critically is usually given the label "Islamophobic." Politicians assure us that "Islam is a religion of peace." Liberal theologians explain that "Muslims worship the same God as Jews and Christians." Politicians assure us that "Sharia law poses no threat to our

Constitution." It is difficult to see clearly in the midst of this fog of political correctness.

It is important to understand Islam in light of world missions. Just a few decades ago, most of the closed countries were communist countries. Some of those countries today are still closed, but many more are open to missionaries. Today the really closed countries to missions are the Muslim countries. Moreover, most of these Muslim countries lie in the so-called "10/40 Window" (so named because the countries are located between 10 and 40 degrees north of the equator). Churches and mission organizations want to focus greater evangelistic outreach in this area of the world.

More than a decade ago, I wrote a book on the subject of Islam that is now out of print. It seemed like a good time to add new material and update existing material. Some of this information comes using radio interviews that I have conducted with experts. Other material comes from my daily "Viewpoints" commentary available through the Point of View radio talk show.

These short chapters are my attempt to help you understand Islam and terrorism. We will describe the history and structure of Islam. We will examine the theology of Islam. We will also talk about how to witness to other Muslims. We will even look at the crusades and the current clash of civilizations between Islam and the west. And we will detail the challenges of Muslim terrorism and how our country and other countries must respond.

# SECTION 1 History and Theology

A religion takes on the attributes and characteristics of its founder. That is certainly the case with Islam and Muhammad. What is his history? What are the beliefs and theology of most Muslims in the world today? What are the major divisions of Islam?

# CHAPTER 1 – THE HISTORY OF ISLAM

Any social or political movement usually takes on the attributes and characteristics of its founder. That is also true of a religion. In order to understand the Muslim religion, we need to begin with Muhammad.

Islam is a monotheistic religion based upon the holy book, the Qur'an, which its followers believe was sent by God through the angel Gabriel to the prophet Muhammad. Additional teachings are also recorded in the Hadith.

The foundational belief of Islam is the monotheistic belief that God is one. In Arabic, God is called Allah. The name Allah was used before the time of Muhammad and does not specify any gender. Because Islam teaches the unity of God, Muslims reject the Christian doctrine of the trinity of God. Muslims also reject the Eastern religions that teach polytheism.

## History of Muhammad

Muhammad was born in 570 into the Quraysh tribe that had the responsibility of maintaining the Ka'bah (a stone used in pagan rituals in Mecca). His father died almost six months before he was born, and his mother died when he was six years old. So, his grandfather reared him until he died when Muhammad was eight. Finally, his uncle became his custodian. During his teen years, he followed his uncle on trips to Syria to trade goods. Overall, Muhammad lived a normal life, except that he never participated in the pagan rituals in Mecca.

After his years of traveling with his uncle, Muhammad became a merchant. As a young man, Muhammad obtained the patronage of Khadija. At age 25, he married this wealthy widow merchant who was 15 years his senior. He led her trade caravans all over the Arabian Peninsula and as far away as Damascus. They had five children together.

When he was 40 years of age, Muhammad had a vision. Sometimes he would retire to a cave on Mount Hira (outside Mecca) for relaxation. In 610, he said he received a vision from the angel Gabriel during the month of Ramadan. At first, he wondered about its source, but his wife Khadijah (and others) believed he was a prophet. After his first revelation, Muhammad did not receive another for nearly three years. During that time, he became despondent and doubted whether Allah was pleased with his conduct.

He did begin to have additional revelations until his death, and these messages were later compiled and recorded in the Qur'an. Over time, some of the revelations of Muhammad became more unusual. He claimed to speak to the dead and even prayed for the dead at one cemetery. He also received revelation from both Allah and Satan. Perhaps the most famous of these are the so-called "Satanic Verses."

Muhammad began preaching against the greed, economic oppression, and idolatry of his time. He also preached against the polytheism of the Arab tribes and called on the many factions of the Arab peoples to unite under the worship of Allah. Muhammad proclaimed to those in Mecca that they were worshipping false gods and idols. This preaching was not only controversial, but it began to affect the commercial interests of those who profited from the worship at the Ka'bah in Mecca. Even his own tribe turned against him. He and his followers came under persecution.

Although some joined Muhammad, most of the residents either ignored him or criticized him. His message was not well received even by his Quraysh brethren in Mecca. It is at that point that Muhammad's rage surfaced. When even his uncle, Abu Lahab, rejected his message, Muhammad cursed him and his wife in violent language: "May the hands of Abu Lahab perish! May he himself perish! Nothing shall his wealth and gains avail him. He shall be burnt in a flaming fire, and his wife, laden with faggots, shall have a rope of fiber around her neck!" (Sura 111:1-5).

In 620, Muhammad claimed that he experienced a night journey with the angel Gabriel that took him from Mecca to a far land (later Muslims said this was Jerusalem – the location which today is known as the Dome of the Rock). He also said he traveled to both heaven and hell and spoke with previous prophets such as Abraham, Moses, and Jesus. He led them in prayer and then returned to Mecca.

His wife and uncle died in 619, and he married another woman. Tensions were rising, and even his own tribe refused to protect him. Various threats were made against his life. Some of his followers actually fled to a nearby Christian king for protection.

The leaders in Mecca were growing even more concerned about the influence of Muhammad and his followers. So, they devised a plan to assassinate Muhammad in order to rid their city of him and Muslim followers. Muhammad and his small Muslim community eventually fled from Mecca in 622 to Medina (a small agricultural oasis to the north of Mecca) where a band of tribal warriors accepted his role as prophet. This flight (known as the *Hijra*) marks the beginning of the Muslim calendar. This is why Muslim dates have the designation AH (After Hijra).

## Muhammad in Medina

While in Medina, Muhammad began to organize various aspects of Islam. He proposed that the Muslim holy day would be on Friday so that it would not conflict with the Jewish Sabbath. Originally, Muslims prayed toward Jerusalem, but that was later changed to Mecca. He also adopted Abraham as the patriarch of the Muslim faith but considered him the father of the Arabs through Ishmael.

Muhammad also established what could be considered the foundational document of Islam. It declared that the community of Muslim believers as the *umma* and set forth the strictures under which they would live. This brotherhood of believers replaced the brotherhood of the tribes. They were to be governed by the Muslim theocracy in which all institutions were subservient to the religion.

During this time, he built a mosque in Medina and established the pillars of Islam that exist even to this day. These include the confession, prayer, almsgiving, fasting, and a pilgrimage.

Muhammad also divided the world into two spheres: dar al-Islam (the house of submission – Islam) and dar al-Harb (the house of war). The first is government by Islamic law and tradition. The second is outside Muslim rule.

While they were in Medina, Muhammad and his fellow Muslims raided caravans and engaged in a number of battles with his growing army of followers. Although most of these battles were with those from Mecca who rejected his teaching, some were against the Jews. In one particular battle with the last Jewish tribe in Medina, he and his followers killed 600-800 Jewish men and took the wives and children as booty.

Because he was raiding caravans from Mecca, relations between Mecca and Muhammad grew worse. After Muhammad led a raid on a Meccan caravan in 624, the leaders in Mecca decided to send an army to Medina to defeat Muhammad and his followers.

This was a major turning point in the life of Muhammad in what is now called the battle of Badr. Even though they were outnumbered three-to-one, his Muslim troops were able to defeat the Quraysh. This appeared to be a divine authentication of the blessing of Allah on the teaching of Muhammad. He also attributed the victory to Allah sending angels. He also said that similar help would come to Muslims who remained faithful to Allah.

> Allah had helped you at Badr, when ye were a contemptible little force; then fear Allah: thus, may you show your gratitude. Remember thou saidst to the Faithful: 'Is it not enough for you that Allah should help you with three thousand angels specially sent down?' Yes, if ye remain firm, and act aright, even if the enemy should rush here on you in hot haste, your Lord would help you with five thousand angels making a terrific onslaught (Sura 3:123-125).

The victory at Badr also posed a problem: the spoils of war. One of the chapters of the Qur'an actually spells out the distribution of this booty: "And know that whatever ye take as spoils of war, lo! a fifth thereof is for Allah, and for the messenger and for the kinsman (who hath need) and orphans and the needy and the wayfarer, if ye believe in Allah and that which We revealed unto Our slave on the Day of Discrimination, that day when the two armies met" (Sura 8:41).

By 628, the Muslim army was so strong that Muhammad decided to return to Mecca as a pilgrim. Even though he was not allowed to finish his pilgrimage, he did sign a treaty that would allow Muslims to make a pilgrimage to Mecca the next year.

In 630, Muhammad assembled an army of 10,000 men and returned to Mecca and took the city without much bloodshed. Most of the Meccans converted to Islam, and others saw the wisdom of not resisting this new powerful religious and military leader. Four people were executed, one a woman who wrote satirical lyrics about Muhammad. He demanded a pledge of allegiance from the citizens of Mecca to him and his religion. Muhammad also destroyed the idols in the shrine in Mecca (known as the Ka'bah) and instituted the practices of Islam in the holy city of Mecca.

Muhammad now had control of both Medina and Mecca, which was the economic and religious center of the Arabian Peninsula. He then decided to return to Medina, a city that came to be known as the "City of the Prophet." And he continued to expand his sphere of political and religious influence in the Arabian Peninsula for the next two years. He was at the pinnacle of his power, and then he died in 632. But rather than that being the end of Islam, it began an incredible expansion both to the east to Persia and to the west through Northern Africa and into Spain.

## After Muhammad's Death

When Muhammad died, the remaining Muslims faced a challenge. Who would lead them? Should they choose one person to lead them or separate into many communities? Who would be their leader and spokesman?

The Muslim leaders picked Abu Bakr (Muhammad's father-in-law and early supporter). He was chosen to assume the role of caliph or successor to Muhammad. However, many who submitted to Muhammad refused to submit to the leadership of

Abu Bakr. Several tribes wanted political independence; some sought to break religiously as well. The result was what has come to be known as the Apostasy wars. After two years of fighting to put down both religious and political threats, Abu Bakr extended his control to include the entire Arabian Peninsula. Islam was now in a position to extend its influence beyond Arabia with a large standing army of believers.

The leaders that emerged from this period were known as caliphs. The first four caliphs were companions of Muhammad. During this same period, Muslim armies began to conquer the Persian Empire to the east and began to take control of the North African and Syrian territories of the Byzantine Empire. In a fairly short period of time, Islam was transformed from a religion of a small city-state in the Arabian Peninsula into a major world religion that covered the land from northwest Africa to central Asia.

The third caliph (whose name was Uthman and was responsible for collecting the variant versions of the Qur'an) was murdered by troops who mutinied over matters of pay and privileges. These troops and others in Medina declared the new caliph to be Ali, (who was a cousin of Muhammad who was an early convert and also the husband of Muhammad's daughter).

This lead to the split between two major groups in Islam: Sunni and Shi'ite. The Shi'ite Muslim tradition believes that Muhammad designated Ali as his successor. Ali faced a major military threat from other Muslims and fought a battle and later agreed

20

to arbitration. When he was killed in 661, most Muslims accepted the leadership of one of the caliphs. But the division between two sects of Islam was now established. Even during these civil wars, the world of Islam continued to expand and dominate the region. In many ways, this new Muslim state became the successor to the empires of Rome and Persia. The Muslim empire spanned from Spain in the west to India in the east. In the centuries that followed, Islam penetrated deeper into Africa and Asia, extending as far as the Philippines.

This time period was the beginning of the golden age of Islam, which produced some of the world's finest philosophers and mathematicians. Baghdad, for example, had a library unmatched by anything else in the world and housed writings from Plato and Aristotle.

Also during this time, conflict between Islam and Christianity erupted. In 691, the Dome of the Rock Mosque was erected in Jerusalem. In 715 the Great Mosque was built in Damascus. So, by 1095, a series of Crusades were begun in an effort to reclaim the Holy Land from the Muslims.

By the tenth century, the power of the caliphs was reduced as power shifted to the military commanders, who frequently took the title of sultan (meaning authority). Much of this military leadership was Turkish.

From the tenth to the sixteenth century, the size of the Muslim world nearly doubled. This expansion was not so much due to the military conquering lands as it was due to traveling merchants and itinerant preachers. Teachers of a devotional life also developed during this time. This would include the sect of Islam known as Sufism.

From the sixteenth century onward, Islam began to be affected by the influence of European powers. Eventually, European countries colonized much of the Muslim world. This situation remained relatively unchanged until the end of WWI. Much of the map of the Middle East was drawn up, and later many of the Muslim countries gained political independence. The discovery and development of the vast oil reserves in many Muslim lands have also brought economic independence.

Today Islam is the second largest religion in the world with approximately 1.6 billion adherents worldwide. It is also one of the fastest growing religions in the world. The Islam religion can be found around the globe. Islam is no longer just a religion of the Middle East. There are actually more Muslims in Asia (60 percent) than in the Arab world (22 percent) and sub-Saharan Africa (12 percent). The country with the most Muslims today is not an Arab country but Indonesia in Southeast Asia.

# CHAPTER 2 – THE BELIEFS OF ISLAM

Since there are more than a billion and a half Muslims in the world, it is not surprising that the beliefs of Muslims are quite diverse. Most Muslims accept the following six basic religious articles of faith.

The first basic belief is that there is no God but Allah. Before Muhammad came on the scene, the Arabs in that region were polytheists. Muhammad taught that they should devote themselves solely to the chief God of the pantheon whose name was Allah. To worship any other deity is considered shirk or blasphemy.

The second article of faith is a belief in angels and jinn. The Muslim belief in angels is in many ways similar to the Christian belief. According to Islam, two angels are believed to accompany every Muslim, one on the right to record his good deeds, and one on the left to record his evil deeds. Jinn is not the same as the belief in demons. Jinn is actually spirit beings capable of both good and evil actions. They also have the ability to take possession of human beings.

The third article is belief in God's holy books. There are 104 holy books that are mentioned in the Qur'an. The major books include the Law given to Moses, the Psalms given to David, the Gospel (or Injil) given to Jesus, and the Qur'an given to

23

Muhammad. Islam teaches that each of these communicates the same basic message of God's will to man. But even a cursory reading of these will find major discrepancies between the Bible and the Qur'an. Islam teaches that these differences arose because the Bible has been corrupted in its transmission to us.

Muslims also believe in a number of God's prophets. While they do believe there were many prophets, there is no agreement as to how many prophets there have been. Some writers say that there were hundreds of thousands of prophets. Some who are considered prophets are: Adam, Noah, Abraham, Moses, and Jesus. All Muslims agree that Muhammad was God's final and supreme prophet. He is referred to as the "seal" of the prophets (Sura 33:40). Though Muhammad even writes in the Qur'an that he was a sinner, there are still many Muslims throughout the world who come close to worshiping him.

Predestination is a fifth article of faith. A frequent expression among Muslims is *inshallah*, which means, "if Allah wills." This is essentially a belief in predestination (*qadar*). Allah is the sovereign ruler of the universe. Whatever He wills comes to pass.

Allah is directing the fate of each individual according to his divine will. Although some Muslims have modified this doctrine of predestination in their teachings, the Qur'an appears to support the idea that all things (both good and evil) are the direct result of God's will. Those who conclude that Islam is a fatalistic religion have a good reason for doing so.

On the other hand, the Qur'an also teaches that believers are to follow the straight path (Sura 1:6). Therefore they are responsible for their actions. They must do what Allah commands in order to please him and be admitted into paradise. Muslims must obey the five pillars of Islam in order to achieve this reward.

The final article of faith is belief in a final judgment. According to Islam, Allah will judge the works of all men at the end of history. Those whose good deeds outweigh their bad deeds will enter into paradise. All others will be consigned to hell. Essentially Islam is a works-oriented salvation where a person's good works become the means to salvation.

## The Five Pillars of Islam

Although the beliefs of Muslims vary, all believe in what is called the "Five Pillars of Islam." These provide an accurate summary of the practices of this religion.

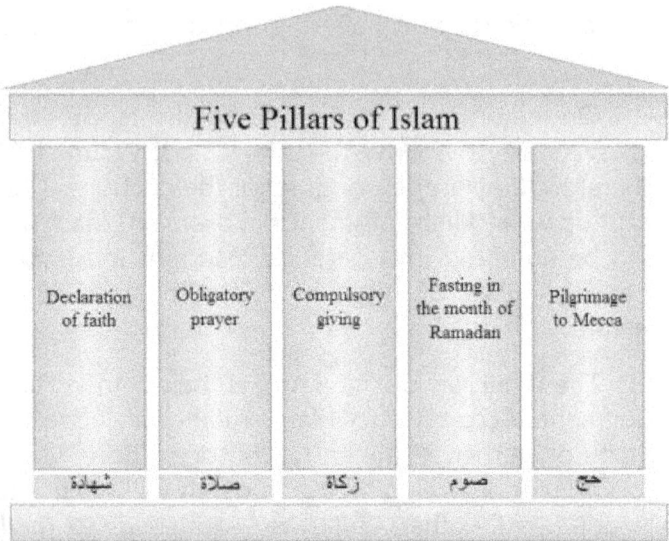

Five Pillars of Islam

| Declaration of faith | Obligatory prayer | Compulsory giving | Fasting in the month of Ramadan | Pilgrimage to Mecca |
|---|---|---|---|---|
| شهادة | صلاة | زكاة | صوم | حج |

1. *Shahadah*: The first pillar is recitation of the creed: "There is no God but Allah, and Muhammad is the prophet of Allah." It can be found in many passages within the Qur'an (Sura 3:81; 5:83-84; 2:255; 3:18; 3:144; 4:87; 7:172; 33:40; 48:29; 64:8).

This statement is the foundation for all other beliefs in Islam. It is what makes someone a Muslim. These words are whispered into the ears of a Muslim both at birth and at death. Muslims repeat the *Shahadah* in prayer (spoken fourteen times a day in the ritual prayers). Those who convert to Islam are to recite the creed. It is generally believed that you must recite this creed in the presence of two witnesses in order to formally convert to Islam. But conversion involves more than mere intellectual assent to the creed. The devout Muslim must unite belief (imam) with practice (din).

2. *Salat*: The second pillar is the daily practice of prayer. Muslim prayers are vocal, orderly, and directional. They may be done individually or in community, but they are required five times each day (dawn and sunrise, noon and mid-afternoon, mid-afternoon to sunset, sunset to twilight, and from twilight to dawn).

The daily prayers must be voiced in Arabic as the follower of Islam faces toward Mecca. Words and gestures are specific as Muslims line up in orderly rows (Sura 2:3, 117; 11:114; 17:78; 20:14, 130; 30:17-18). Men and women are segregated within the mosque. A Muslim stands and kneels during prayer, and these actions are called rakahs.

The central prayer for Muslims is the Fatiha, which many have compared to the Lord's Prayer in Christianity. It is said out load during the daily times of prayer, as well as on special occasions. "In the name of Allah, Most Gracious, Most Merciful. Praise be to Allah the Cherisher and Sustainer of the Worlds. Most Gracious, Most Merciful; Master of the Day of Judgment. Thee do we worship, and Thine aid we seek. Show us the straight path" (Sura 1:1-6).

In Muslim and Western countries where there is a mosque, a prayer leader climbs to the top of the minaret in the mosque and calls the believers to prayer. He chants in Arabic, "God is great. There is no god but Allah, and Muhammad is the messenger of Allah. Come to prayer. Come to prayer. Come to success in this life and the hereafter." Within the mosque, there is water for absolution. Before prayer, Muslims washes their hands, forearms, face, and feet. They also clean the nose and rinse the mouth.

3. *Zakat*: The third pillar is almsgiving which is mandated giving to the poor and needy within society (Sura 2:43, 83, 110, 177, 277; 9:60; 103; 24:56; 27:3; 57:7; 59:7; 98:5). Born an orphan himself, Muhammad was deeply concerned for the needy. A Muslim must first recognize that everything is the property of Allah. The Qur'an requires that each Muslim give 2.5 percent of one's income to the poor or to the spread of Islam. The collected funds are used for building and supporting mosques, for printing the Qur'an, and for the advancement of Islam.

4. *Sawm*: The fourth pillar of Islam is the fast during the month of Ramadan (Sura 2:183-185). This is during the ninth lunar month of the Muslim calendar. This is significant in the Muslim calendar for two reasons. First, this is the time when Muhammad is said to have received the first of his revelations from God. It is also the time when he and his followers made their historic trek from Mecca to Medina.

During this month, Muslims in good health are required to abstain from all food, drink, smoking, and sexual intercourse during daylight hours. In its place, Muslims are to read the Qur'an meditatively and introspectively. The Qur'an has been divided into thirty equal parts for reading during this time. This month-long fast promotes the Muslim's self-discipline, dependence on Allah, and compassion for the needy. The festival of Eid al-Fitr (breaking the fast) is held at the end of Ramadan as a time of celebration for adhering to the fast. This includes visitations, meetings, and meals.

5. *Hajj*: The fifth pillar is a pilgrimage to Mecca that occurs during the last month of the Muslim year. Every able-bodied Muslim is to make a pilgrimage to Mecca once during his life (Sura 2:196-201; 3:97; 22:26-29). Pilgrims travel to Mecca, which is the holiest city in Islam and the birthplace of Muhammad. Only Muslims may enter Mecca.

The focal point of Mecca is the Ka'bah which is an ancient stone building (thirty feet wide and forty feet long). A black stone (believed to be a meteorite) is set in the corner. The Ka'bah existed before the time of Muhammad. He taught that their worship had been corrupted and removed the 360 idols from the Ka'bah and instituted Muslim worship of Allah in its place.

Those who make the pilgrimage must circle the Ka'bah seven times, run seven times between the two hills of Mecca, as well as travel thirteen miles to the place where Muhammad preached his last sermon and throw seven stones at the Devil at another site. Many of these elements of the prescribed activity during the pilgrimage pre-date Islam and are of pagan origin.

## A Sixth Pillar of Islam?

Many Muslims believe there are not five pillars of Islam but actually six pillars. That sixth pillar is jihad. There are over 100 verses in the Qur'an that call upon Muslims to wage a war of jihad against infidels.

The word jihad is actually the noun of the Arabic verb jahidi, which means to "strive hard." This verse is an example: "O Prophet! Strive hard against the unbelievers and the hypocrites, and be firm against them. Their abode is Hell, and evil refuge indeed (Sura 9:73).

Although some Muslims understand this striving to be merely intellectual and philosophical, the usual translation of jihad involves a holy war. That has been the traditional interpretation since the time of Muhammad.

Bernard Lewis is the professor of Near Eastern Studies at Princeton University and a leading authority on Islam. He says that "The more common interpretation, and that of the overwhelming majority of the classical jurists and commentators, presents jihad as armed struggle for Islam against infidels and apostates."[1]

Jihad was to be waged on the battlefield: "When you meet the unbelievers in the battlefield, strike off their heads and, when you have laid them low, bind your captives firmly" (Sura 47:4).

Consider some of these other passages concerning jihad. Faithful Muslims wage jihad against unbelievers: "O ye who believe! Fight the unbelievers who gird your about, and let them find firmness in you; and know that Allah is with those who fear Him" (Sura 9:123).

Muslims are also to wage jihad not only against unbelievers but against those who have strayed from the faith: "Prophet, make war on the unbelievers and

---

[1] Bernard Lewis, "Jihad vs. Crusade," *Wall Street Journal*, 27 September 2001.

the hypocrites and deal rigorously with them. Hell shall be their home: and evil fate" (Sura 9:73).

Ultimately, they are fighting against Satan and his allies: "Those who believe fight in the cause of Allah, and those who reject faith fight in the cause of evil: so fight ye against the friends of Satan" (Sura 4:76).

Often when these various verses of the sword from the Qur'an are cited, skeptics wonder if these are just a few isolated verses or if they are quoted out of context. How can we answer this question?

First, these are not isolated passages in the Qur'an, but can be found throughout the book. In fact, there are over 100 verses of the sword that advocate jihad in the Qur'an. Many of these verses are found in Sura 9. This was the last chapter communicated by Muhammad and illustrates his desire to use the sword and other forms of violence to spread the religion of Islam.

Second, let's consider the context. While some will argue that these verses were intended only for the time of Muhammad, there is nothing within the Qur'an to justify such an interpretation. Nowhere within the Qur'an is there any restriction placed on these verses of the sword.

Third, these passages are used today by leaders of jihad warfare. They may call upon true believers to engage in warfare, terrorism, assassination, or persecution of unbelievers. For example, Osama bin Laden quoted from Sura 9:14 ("Fight them, and Allah will punish them by your hands, cover them with shame") in a videotape found in Afghanistan by the U.S. Army.

## Other Verses

While the Qur'an is the foundational book in Islam, there is also the Hadith. It is a collection of the sayings of Muhammad and is considered the second most important book in Islam. In the Hadith, we get additional perspectives on jihad. Here are four examples:

• "Allah's apostle said, 'Know that paradise is under the shades of swords." – Hadith 4:55

• "Allah's apostle said, 'I have been ordered to fight with the people till they say, "None has the right to be worshipped but Allah," and whoever says, "None has the right to be worshipped but Allah," his life and property will be saved by men.'" – Hadith 4:125

• "It is not fitting for a prophet that he should have prisoners of war [and free them with ransom] until he has made a great slaughter [among his enemies] in the land." – Hadith 4:161.

• "Whoever changed his Islamic religion, then kill him." – Hadith 9:45

## Martyrdom and Suicide Bombers

In Islam, a martyr is called a *shaheed* (meaning witness). The concept of the shaheed is not found in the Qur'an but a discussion can be found in the Hadith.

Muslims who die in a holy war (*jihad bis saif*) are usually considered a martyr in Islam. This would be different than a suicide bomber. Some Muslims would consider a suicide bomber a martyr, but other Muslims would not consider them a martyr since there are strict admonitions in Islam against suicide. These Muslims would consider such actions as contrary to the teachings of Muhammad.

The Qur'an does teach that those who die in a holy war against infidels will be admitted into paradise (Sura 47:4-6) because Allah will not forget their deeds. The Hadith expands upon this and promotes martyrdom and promises rewards in heaven.

## The Major Divisions of Islam

Islam is not a monolithic system. Though all Muslims draw their inspiration from Muhammad and the teachings in the Qur'an, there are many identifiable groups and movements within Islam.

The most significant division is between Sunni and Shi'a Islam. The Sunnis comprise about eighty to ninety percent of all Muslims. They draw their name from the fact that they look both to the Qur'an and to the "Sunna" in establishing proper Muslim conduct. The Sunna is the recorded behavior or example of Muhammad and of the early Muslim community. There are many sub-divisions among the Sunnis, but they all identify themselves as Sunni.

Sunnis currently control the holy cities of Mecca and Medina. They adhere to the five pillars of Islam and take a strong stand on the successor to

Muhammad. They believe the successor must be a male from the Quraysh tribe. This leader will be the caliph who will govern Islam and provide theological direction to all Muslims, including the interpretation of sharia law. These caliphs have ruled continuously until the Ottoman Empire fell.

The other major group of Muslims is the Shi'ites. They comprise about ten percent of all Muslims. They reside mainly in southern Iraq and in Iran. The word Shi'ite means "partisan," and refers to the fact that Shi'ites are "partisans of Ali." As we have noted, Ali was the son-in-law and cousin of Muhammad and one of the early Caliphs. The Shi'ites believe that the leader of Islam should be a descendant of Ali, whom they believe possess a special divine anointing for this task. The Muslim leaders selected Abu Bakr as the first caliph. Instead, Ali was selected the fourth caliph, but Shiites consider him the first imam.

When conflicts arose, Ali was killed. His body is buried in Iraq and has become a great Shi'ite shrine. According to the Shi'ite teaching, pilgrimage to this shrine provides forgiveness for present and past sins.

Shi'ites are a majority in only a few Muslim countries (Iran, Iraq, Azerbaijan, and Bahrain). They are various sects of Shia including one branch known as the "Twelvers." They believe in twelve imams who linked God and man after Muhammad's death. The first imam was Ali, and the twelfth imam was Mahdi. According to the the Twelvers, Mahdi was taken by God into hiding from his enemies in 870. They also believe that the boy never died and will return to earth bringing justice at the end of days. Until his return, Shiites believe that an ayatollah may rule in his place. They also believe that the ayatollah is infallible. There have been a number of ayatollahs in the Shiite country of Iran.

There are a few other differences between Sunnis and Shi'ites. For example,

Shi'ites differ from Sunnis in the way they hold their hands during prayer. Shiites also commemorate the death of the third imam, Hussein, who was beheaded by the Sunni Army in 680. Some of the Shi'ite pilgrims visit his shrine and men dressed in white beat themselves until they bleed as penance for those who left him to be killed.

Some of the violence between Sunnis and Shi'ites in Iraq surfaced after the first Gulf War. The U.S. encouraged the Shi'ites to rise up against Saddam Hussein and the Sunnis. He retaliated by eradicating entire districts. Shiites believe they have a score to settle with the Sunni minority that oppressed them.

A third group of Muslims are the Sufis. They seek a mystical experience of God, rather than a merely intellectual knowledge of Him, and who also are given to a number of superstitious practices.

Sufi Muslims are the mystics in Islam. They believe that the soul can rise to Allah during prayer and other spiritual exercises. Although they also read the Qur'an, they read it in a different way than other Muslims. They believe that it is an allegory of our soul's union with Allah. They, therefore, follow an inward path (tariqa) in their faith.

The word "sufi" means purity and comes from the fact that the first Sufis wore white, and they withdrew from society to practice their ascetic lifestyle. They use various spiritual exercises in an attempt to experience God directly. Perhaps the best-known example of Sufis would be the "whirling dervishes" who spin around and repeat the name of Allah as they dance.

## Wahhabi Muslims

Wahhabism is a movement within Sunni Islam that was founded in the eighteenth century by Muhammad ibn 'Abd al- Wahhab who established a form of Muslim literalism that flourishes today in Saudi Arabia. He and his followers attempted to purify Islam and return it to its Muslim roots and pursue the literal interpretation of the Qur'an. Wahhab aggressively fought for purity within Islam by burning books, destroying Muslim holy places, and killing Muslims who disagreed with him.

The influence of Wahhabism on the Saudis provided a platform for this sect of Islam to gain national and international attention. When the Saudi forces conquered Arabia in 1925, they took control of Islam's two most holy cities: Mecca and Medina. This provided them with a strong religious platform because of the annual pilgrimages to Mecca each year.

The oil money of Saudi Arabia provided the financial platform. Wahhabism became the "official, state-enforced doctrine of one of the most influential governments in all Islam."  The Saudi oil money helped to fund Wahhabi propagation of their views at home and abroad.

How influential is Wahhabism? It was the primary influence on Osama bin Laden and all of the 9/11 hijackers. It was also influential in the theology of the Taliban in Afghanistan. Bernard Lewis uses this analogy to illustrate the influence of Wahhabism. He says, imagine that the Ku Klux Klan or a similar group took control of Texas and its oil. Then imagine what they could do with this money to propagate their version of "Christianity" through heavily endowed schools and colleges.[2]

During the Soviet occupation of Afghanistan, the Wahhabi soldiers fought the Soviets in Afghanistan in the 1980s, with U.S. support. There, Wahhabis linked with radical followers of Sayyid Qutb. One commentator said that alliance was like "mixing nitroglycerin in a blender." The result was a more militant strain of Wahhabism that had an emphasis on taking the fight to outsiders (e.g., the infidels and the West).

## The Significance of Mecca

Mecca is the holiest city within the religion of Islam and is the place where the Sacred Mosque (al-Masjid al-Haram) is found. In fact, Mecca is considered so holy that non-Muslims are not permitted to enter the city. It is considered holy because it is the birthplace of Muhammad and the place where he first began to teach from his recitations (the Qur'an).

---

[2] Bernard Lewis, *The Crisis of Islam: Holy War and the Unholy Terror* (NY: The Modern Library, 2003), 129.

The Qur'an also teaches that it is the place where Abraham was supposed to sacrifice Ishmael. This teaching is contrary to the biblical teaching that he was supposed to sacrifice Isaac on Mount Moriah.

Mecca is also the object of every Muslim's prayer. Each day over 1 billion Muslims prays five times as they face in the direction of Mecca. All able-bodied Muslims who can afford to go are commanded to make a pilgrimage once during their lifetime.

The Ka'bah is a small cubical building within the Sacred Mosque. Muslims claim that Abraham built the Ka'bah. Even before the birth of Muhammad, religious activities took place at the Ka'bah. It was a shrine and trading center for many generations. When Muhammad returned to Mecca, he removed the religious idols from the Ka'bah and dedicated it as the center of worship.

Muslims gather for their pilgrimage to Mecca (known as the Hajj) during the month of Dhu al-Hijjah. The primary focus is the Ka'bah. While they are there, pilgrims must circle the Ka'bah seven times. Many will try to kiss or touch its cornerstone.

Pilgrims also drink from the well of Zamzam and often bring back a bottle of this water. The water supposedly has special properties and health benefits.

They also travel to a small village where there are stone columns that symbolize the Devil. They throw stones at these columns. They also travel to the Hill of Arafat for prayer. This is the traditional site of Muhammad's farewell sermon.

# CHAPTER 3 – THE THEOLOGY OF ISLAM

Islam involves both doctrine (beliefs) and duties (practice). Muslims are to believe and act according to the revelation given to Muhammad and written down in the Qur'an. They are to do this as an act of submission to the will of Allah. After all, the word *Islam* means "submission" and the word *Muslim* describes someone who submits.

The basic theology of Islam, therefore, can be found primarily within the Qur'an because it is the foundational religious text of Islam. Islam teaches that the Qur'an contains the words of Allah, and the "mother of the book" is actually in heaven with Allah (13:39; 43:3-4; 85:21-23). It is composed of the revelations to Muhammad over a twenty-three-year period and was later compiled in the years 646-650 from materials written by Muhammad before his death in 632. Muslims regard it as Allah's final revelation to mankind.

The Arabic word *Qur'an* is the noun form of the Arabic verb *qara'a*, which means "to recite." When the angel Gabriel appeared, he commanded Muhammad three separate times to "recite." Sura 12:2 says, "We have sent it down as an Arabic Qur'an, in order that ye may learn wisdom." The Qur'an is the collection of those recitations revealed to Muhammad in Arabic. Muslims believe that only the Qur'an in Arabic is the true revelation. Thus, the only way to understand the revelation is in the original Arabic language. For that reason, an English translation of the Qur'an is seen as merely an interpretation and not considered a real Qur'an. They may be helpful for personal use but have no weight in any religious debate or discussion.

The Qur'an consists of 114 chapters (or suras) that include 6,616 verses (ayas). Of these chapters, 86 were written in Mecca and 28 were written in Medina. The Qur'an is about 1/3 the size of the Bible. Unlike the Bible, the Qur'an is not in chronological order. With the exception of the first chapter, the rest of the chapters are ordered with the longest chapters first. As it turns out, the Qur'an is almost in reverse chronological order. That has caused some to suggest that it could be read from back to front in order to understand the progression of the revelation.

Like the Bible, the Qur'an claims to be divine inspiration. Islam teaches that the Qur'an is a word-for-word copy of God's final revelation supposedly sent down from heaven during the month of Ramadan, during the night of power (Sura 17:85). This was supposedly revealed to Muhammad through the angel Gabriel (Sura 25:32).

Muslims believe that the Qur'an was divinely revealed in its present state without corruption. Thus, Islam does not allow literary criticism or historical criticism. In essence, the Qur'an is to be read and memorized, but not to be questioned (Sura 5:101).

Muslims show great respect for the Qur'an because they believe it to be the perfect revelation from Allah. For example, they will kiss the book and even touch it to their forehead. And they will also store the Qur'an on the highest shelf in their house.

The transmission of the Qur'an is fairly simple. After Muhammad's death, Caliph Abu Bakr collected the recitations into one document based on the memorization of Muhammad's companions. Later (in 652) Caliph Uthman established the authorized version of the Qur'an and burned all the other conflicting versions.

In addition to the Qur'an, there is the Hadith which provides a narration of Muhammad's life and is important is determining the Sunnah or Muslim way of life. The Hadith is a collection of: (1) what Muhammad said (qawl), (2) what Muhammad did (fi'l), and (3) what Muhammad approved (taqrir). These passages provide guidance in how Muslims are to live and behave. Muhammad is the example every faithful Muslim is to follow.

## Qur'an and the Bible

A foundational belief in Islam is that mankind can often be led astray and that humans can be forgetful about God. So, Muhammad taught that God sent various prophets (such as Moses and Jesus) to bring fresh revelation from God.

However, Muhammad also taught that these various revelations had been lost or corrupted. While most Muslims will have respect for the Bible, they will also believe that the Bible has been corrupted in its transmission. Only the Qur'an, they believe, has been perfectly transmitted to us. It is the authentic and authoritative word of Allah.

Both the Bible and the Qur'an claim to be divine revelation. And both books claim to have been accurately preserved through the centuries. But Islam makes a very strong case for that preservation. For example, if you take a tour of an Islamic center, the guide will tell you that the current copy of the Qur'an contains the exact words given by Muhammad to his followers with absolutely no mistakes.

By contrast, Christians do not make quite the same sweeping claim regarding the Bible. While they do affirm that the original manuscripts of the Bible are without error, they do not make the same Muslim claim about the perfect transmission of the Bible. They may believe that the transmission has been extremely accurate, but will not make a claim similar to what many Muslims claim about the Qur'an.

The Bible and the Qur'an disagree with one another on major issues. The two books make contradictory claims about God, Jesus, salvation, and biblical history. Both claims cannot be true. They both could be false, but they cannot both be true because the accounts contradict each other.

Islam solves this dilemma by teaching that the Jews and Christians corrupted the Bible. This is the doctrine of *tahrif*, which is the Arabic word for corruption. That is their explanation for why the Qur'an and the Bible disagree. They believe that the People of the Book have corrupted the Bible.

There is a problem with this view: the Qur'an says many positive and complimentary things about the Bible. Sura 5:44 says, "It was we who revealed the Law to Moses; therein was guidance and light."

Verse 46 goes on to say, "And in their footsteps, We sent Jesus the son of Mary, confirming the Law that has come before him. We sent him the Gospel: therein was guidance and light."

The Qur'an (5:68) has this to say about Jews and Christians: "Say, O People of the Book! Ye have not ground to stand upon unless you stand fast by the Law, the Gospel, and all the revelation that has come to you from your Lord."

Allah tells Muhammad to consider previous revelation (10:94) to Jews and Christians: "If thou wert in doubt as to what we have revealed unto thee, then ask those who have been reading the Book from before thee." It also says in Sura 29:46, "And dispute ye not with the People of the Book, except with means better."

It is important to note that in the early days of Islam, the Bible was held in higher regard than later in its history. Muhammad taught that his revelation was the culmination of other revelation provided by such prophets as Moses and Jesus. Therefore, he encouraged others to read and learn from these previous revelations. Only later did Muslims begin to teach that these were corrupted.

Consider the logical problem this creates. On the one hand, the Qur'an calls the Bible, the "word of God" (Sura 6:115). But on the other hand, Muslims argue that the Old and New Testaments have been corrupted and contend that a lost gospel of Jesus has been replaced with Matthew, Mark, Luke, and John.

Here is the problem with this perspective. First, the Qur'an calls the Bible the word of God, and acknowledges that it is divine revelation. Second, it also teaches that Jesus was a prophet and that his teaching had authority. Finally, Muhammad told Muslims to go to Christians (who had been reading the Bible) to affirm Muhammad's message (Sura 10:94).

Therefore, it appears that Muhammad believed that the Bible in existence in the seventh century was accurate. And the Bible we have in our hands today is the same Bible that existed in the seventh century. So if the Bible in the time of Muhammad was accurate, why isn't today's copy also accurate? This is the problem with Muslims arguing that the Bible has been corrupted.

By contrast, the Qur'an does suffer from textual omissions and even errors. From the time of the death of Muhammad to the time in which the Qur'an was compiled, some of what Muhammad spoke was lost due to the death of his companions who had memorized specific passages. And later when multiple versions of the Qur'an appeared, there was a great controversy among Muslims. The Caliph Uthman ordered Zaid bin Thabit to collect all the copies in use, create a standard version and destroy the rest.

## Contradictions Between the Bible and the Qur'an

The Bible and the Qur'an do contradict each other on many issues. Here are just a few examples:

• The Qur'an teaches (Sura 5:116) that Christians worship three gods: the Father, the Mother (Mary) and the Son (Jesus). But the Bible actually teaches that there is one God in three persons (the Trinity).

• The Qur'an says (Sura 37:100-111) that Abraham was going to sacrifice Ishmael, while the Bible teaches that Abraham was going to sacrifice Isaac.

• The Qur'an teaches (Sura 4:157) that Jesus was not crucified. The Bible teaches that Jesus Christ was crucified on a cross.

Many of the statements in the Qur'an are also at odds with historical facts that can be verified through historical accounts.

• The Qur'an says (Sura 20:85-97) that the Samaritans tricked the Israelites at the Exodus and were the ones who built the golden calf. For the record, the word *Samaritan* wasn't even used until 722 B.C. and is several hundred years after the Exodus.

• The Qur'an also states (Sura 18:89-98) that Alexander the Great was a Muslim who worshiped Allah. Alexander lived from 356 B.C. to 323 B.C. hundreds of years *before* Muhammad proclaimed his revelation which became the religion of Islam.

## Islamic Monotheism

The most foundational doctrine in Islam is monotheism. This doctrine is encapsulated in the creed: "There is no God but Allah, and Muhammad is the prophet of Allah." And not only is it a creed, but it is also a statement of faith that routinely heard from the lips of every faithful Muslim. It is the creed by which every Muslim is called to prayer five times a day.

Allah is the name of the God of Islam. And it is important to note that this name for God was known even before the beginning of Islam. In fact, Muhammad's own father bore the name Abd-Allah. Before the time of Muhammad, the tribes in the Arabian Peninsula worshipped many gods. Muhammad taught that there was one true God. Allah literally means "the God." He is one and transcendent. Muhammad proclaimed that all the other deities that were worshiped at the time were not worthy of worship as divine beings.

The Qur'an provides the identity and character of Allah. The first chapter of the Qur'an is known as the Faitha or "opening." It summarizes the foundational belief of Muslims about Allah. According to the passage, he is most gracious and merciful, the sustainer of the world, and master of the Day of Judgment. Therefore, he is to be worshipped (Sura 1:1-7). And in one chapter near the end of the Qur'an (Sura 112), it says, "He is God, One, God the Everlasting Refuge, who has not begotten, and has not been begotten, and equal to Him is not any one."

This passage (along with others in the Qur'an) teaches the absolute unity and sovereignty of Allah. The oneness of God precludes any plural nature to God. And there is no equal to Allah. He is the only God in the heavens, and therefore the only deity worth worshipping and obeying.

The Qur'an teaches that evidence of Allah can be found in creation. There are over eighty passages in the Qur'an that describe the wonders of nature. These all point to the existence of a God who created the heavens and earth. In fact, the Qur'an teaches (Sura 45:3-4) that we can use logic and reason to determine that God exists because He has manifested Himself through the creation.

The Qur'an also teaches that creation can provide theological arguments for the existence of God and the falsity of other deities. Here are a few examples:

• God's is united to His creation (Sura 6:96-100).

• Polytheism and atheism are contrary to reason (Sura 23:119).

• Dualism is self-destructive (Sura 21:22).

Because of this strong emphasis on monotheism, Muslims reject the idea that God could be more than one person or that God could have a partner. The Qur'an teaches the unity of God (*tawhid*). Allah is one God and the same God for all people. Anyone who does not believe this is guilty of the sin of *shirk*. This is the quintessential sin in Islam (Sura 4:48). According to Islam, God cannot have a partner and cannot be joined together in the Godhead with other persons. Muslims, therefore, reject the Christian idea of the Trinity.

Muslims also differ from Christians in their understanding of the nature and character of God. The God of the Bible is knowable. Jesus came into the world that we might know God (John 17:3).

Islam teaches a very different view of God. Allah is transcendent and distant. He is separate from His creation. He is exalted and far removed from mankind. While we may know His will, we cannot know Him personally. In fact, there is very little written about the character of God. Allah is the creator and sustainer of the creation, but He is also unknowable. No person can ever personally know and have a relationship with Allah. Instead, humans are to be in total submission to the will of Allah.

Moreover, Allah does not personally enter into human history. Instead, he deals with the world through His word (the Qur'an), through His prophets (such as Muhammad), and through angels (such as Gabriel).

If you ask a Muslim to describe Allah, most likely they will recite to you a key passage that lists some of the names of God (Sura 59). The Qur'an requires that God is called by these "beautiful names." This passage describes him as: Most Gracious, Most Merciful, The Sovereign, The Holy One, The Guardian of Faith, The Preserver of Safety, The Exalted in Might, etc.

A Muslim will also talk about "the ninety-nine names of Allah." According to tradition, Muhammad said that to memorize and say these ninety-nine names of God will aid a Muslim in entering paradise. Many Muslims even use prayer to help them keep track of the various names of God.

The Muslim perspective on God's love is also very different from the Christian view. Crucial to Christians is the belief that "God so loved the world" (John 3:16).

By contrast, Muslims grow up hearing about all the people Allah does not love:

• "For Allah loves not transgressors" (Sura 2:190).

• "Allah loves not the impious and the sinful" (Sura 2:276).

• "Allah loves not the unbelievers" (Sura 3:32).

• "For Allah loves not the evildoers" (Sura 3:57).

• "Allah loves not the arrogant and boastful men" (Sura 4:36).

### Muslim Belief about Muhammad

Christians frequently make the mistake of assuming that Muhammad has essentially the same role in Islam that Jesus has in Christianity. This is not true. Muslims see Muhammad as a messenger, while Christians see Jesus as *the* message, or the Word (John 1:1).

Muslims believe that Muhammad is the final prophet from Allah. He is referred to as the "seal of the prophets" (Sura 33:40). But while he is revered as a greatest of the prophets, most do not teach that he was sinless. The Qur'an does not make the claim that he was sinless, and there are passages that teach that Muhammad was a man like us (Sura 18:110) and that Allah told Muhammad that he must repent of his sins (Sura 40:55). This differs from the Christian teaching that Jesus Christ lived a perfect and sinless life (2 Cor. 5:21).

But even if Muslims do not see Muhammad as sinless, they do teach that his life should be an example of how they should act. Muhammad's action (known as the sunna) provides a clear path for how Muslims are to behave. One Muslim scholar said, "Know that the key to happiness is to follow the sunna and to imitate the Messenger of God in all his coming and going, his movement and rest, in his way of eating, his attitude, his sleep and his talk."[3]

Muhammad's every action is to be imitated by Muslims. His life is a model for believers. In fact, some Muslims even avoid eating food that Muhammad avoided or never was able to eat.

Muhammad is so revered by Muslims that no attack upon him or even his likeness (e.g., through a cartoon) may be allowed. William Cantrell Smith notes that "Muslims will allow attacks on Allah: there are atheists and atheistic publications, and rationalistic societies; but to disparage Muhammad will provoke from even the most 'liberal' sections of the community a fanaticism of blazing vehemence."[4]

---

[3] Annemarie Schimmel and Abdoldjavad Falaturi, *We Believe in One God* (New York: The Seabury Press, 1979), 31.

[4] Ibid., 35.

## The Qur'an and Jesus

Muslims sometimes accuse Christians of elevating Jesus to an inappropriate level of honor and worship. The Qur'an teaches that Jesus was just a prophet to the Jews. It also teaches that Jesus promoted the coming of Muhammad who is revered as the seal of the prophets.

Muhammad originally portrayed himself as the last of the prophets and showed reverence for the "people of the book." So, Muslims believe many of the same things about Jesus as Christians do:

• The Qur'an refers to Jesus as "the Messiah" or "the Christ" (Sura 4:157). It also calls him "the word of God" (Sura 3:45). He is also called a "spirit" from God (Sura 4:171) and a "sign" (Sura 23:50).

• The Qur'an also teaches that Jesus was born of the virgin Mary. It also says that Jesus performed many miracles, including raising people from the dead.

• The Qur'an also claims that Jesus is alive today. Many Muslims even believe that He will return to earth.

Though Muslims share some Christian beliefs about Jesus, there is two points of disagreement that means a world of difference between Islam and Christianity: Christ's death and deity.

Muslims deny that Jesus was crucified on the cross. They base this on this passage in the Qur'an that talks about what the Jews did to Jesus:

That they said (in boast), 'We killed Christ Jesus, the Son of Mary, the Messenger of Allah'—but they killed him not, crucified him, but so it was made to appear to them, and those who different therein are full of doubts, with no certain) knowledge, but only conjecture to follow, for a surety they killed him not—nay, Allah raised him up to Himself; and Allah is exalted in Power, Wise" (Sura 4:157-158).

Muslims have come to various conclusions about what this means. Perhaps Judas was mistakenly crucified on the cross. Perhaps a disciple volunteered to die on the cross. Maybe God transposed the likeness of Jesus on some poor soul. There are various suggestions that have been made, but they all point to one conclusion: Jesus did NOT die on the cross.

Muslims believe that Jesus never died on the cross in part because they cannot believe that a great prophet of God would ever die a shameful death. Since crucifixion was a humiliating way to die, they believe that God must have intervened so that Jesus would not have to suffer in this way.

They also reject Christ's death on the cross because they reject the Christian idea of original sin and human sinfulness. According to Islam, each person is responsible for his or her actions, and no one else should have to pay for their mistakes. There is no need for Jesus to die on the cross for our sins. There is no need for that atonement. In fact, many Muslims actually claim that the theology of the atonement was interjected into Christianity and has corrupted God's original message of salvation.

53

Muslims not only deny Christ's death, but they deny Christ's deity. While they respect Him as one of the great prophets, they reject the Christian idea that Jesus was God. They reject the biblical doctrine of the trinity, and they reinterpret any biblical passage that might suggest that Jesus and God are the same. The Qur'an teaches that it is blasphemy to equate Jesus with God:

> They do blaspheme who say: "Allah is Christ the son of Mary." But said Christ: "O Children of Israel! Worship Allah, my Lord and your Lord." Whoever joins other gods with Allah, Allah will forbid him the Garden, and the Fire will be his abode. . . .Christ, the son of Mary, was no more than a Messenger; many were the Messengers that passed away before him. His mother was a woman of truth. They had both to eat their (daily) food. See how Allah doth make His signs clear to them; yet see in what ways they are deluded away from the truth! (Sura 5:72, 75)

The Qur'an also teaches that Christians who "call Christ the Son of God" shall face judgment because "Allah's curse" will be upon them (Sura 9:30).

So, it can be said that anyone who accepts the foundational doctrine of Christianity (the Jesus is God) is guilty of the one unforgivable sin within Islam. Essentially the Qur'an teaches that God will forgive any sin except the sin of idolatry (known as *shirk*). Christians are guilty of the one sin that Allah will not forgive.

By contrast, Christianity teaches that we are saved by believing in Jesus as the Son of God. "And the testimony is this, that God has given us eternal life, and this life is in His Son. He who has the Son has the life; he who does not have the Son of God does not have the life. (1 John 5:11-12)"

Jesus claimed to be God, Messiah, and the way to God (Mark 14:61-62; John 10:30; 14:6-9). He also allowed others to worship Him (Matt. 14:33; 28:9; cf. also Acts 10:25-26; 14:12-15). Jesus claimed power over the Sabbath (Matt. 12:8), and he claimed the power to forgive sins (Matt. 9:6, Mark 2:5-10).

### The Prophets

The Qur'an teaches that there have been many prophets in the past leading up to Muhammad (Sura 2:38, 177, 252, 285; 4:80, 164; 17:70; 18:110; 33:40). It actually mentions twenty-five prophets by name, although Islamic tradition suggests there were over 100,000 prophets. Muhammad is the "seal" of the prophets (Sura 33:40) and the "bearer of glad tidings" (Sura 33:45-46).

Jesus is mentioned 97 times in the Qur'an. And the Qur'an emphasizes that the messages of Moses and Jesus are the same as the message of Muhammad (Sura 2:136). The Qur'an teaches that prophets are righteous men who bring the Word of God. They are free from all vices and thus used by God to deliver His message. Muslims routinely say the words "praise be upon him" after the name of every prophet, including Jesus. Within the Qur'an, Jesus is given high honor but not considered the Son of God.

## Angels

According to the Qur'an, angels carry out the commands of Allah (Sura 2:285; 6:100; 34:40-41; 46:29-32; 72:1-28). The most prominent angel in the Qur'an is Gabriel because he is the one who supposedly appeared to Muhammad and provided the revelation. Michael is another angel mentioned in the Qur'an. He is the guardian of the Jews.

The Qur'an also teaches that angels are for our protection: "We are your protectors in this life and in the hereafter" (Sura 41:31; 82:10-12). The Hadith teaches that two angels are assigned to each person at birth: one records good deeds, the other bad deeds. They will give an account of each individual's actions on the Day of Judgment.

Islam also teaches that there is jinn. They are creatures that are invisible and are able to act with free will. Like human beings, they have the capacity to be good or bad. They can take various forms and have the capacity to possess humans. Islamic tradition says that Satan was not an angel but a jinn based upon their understanding of Sura 18:50.

Perhaps the best-known example of jinn can be found in the story of Aladdin in the Western translation of *The Book of One Thousand and One Nights*. He was bound to an oil lamp and granted wishes to whoever freed him from the lamp by polishing it.

## Muslim Belief About Sin

Islam and Christianity have very different views of sin. Although both accept the Genesis account of creation, they come to opposite conclusions.

The Muslim view is that God created Adam and Eve. They sinned, and God forgave them. Unlike Christianity, Islam does not have a doctrine of original sin. Humans do not have a sin nature, but instead are forgetful of God's commands and therefore need prophets to direct them back to His will.

Allah commanded Muhammad to guide humanity back to the path of salvation through obedience to His laws and the performing of good works. Humans need this guidance because they are described in the Qur'an as ignorant, arrogant, and weak-willed.

Sura 2:35-37 has this account of creation: "We said, 'Oh Adam! Dwell thou and thy wife in the Garden, and eat of the bountiful things therein as (where and when) ye will; but approach not this tree, or ye run into harm and transgression.' Then did Satan make them slip from the (Garden), and get them out of the state (of felicity) in what they had been. We said: 'Get ye down all (ye people), with enmity between yourselves. On earth will be your dwelling place.' . . . Then learnt Adam from his Lord words of inspiration, and his Lord turned towards him; for He is oft returning, Most Merciful."

This passage (and others teach) that Adam and Eve disobeyed God's command to them, so God expelled from paradise to earth. In the process, God forgave them. There is no doctrine of the fall, and thus no real need for a savior to take upon Himself the sins of the world.

One Muslim author writes, "Islam teaches that people are born innocent and remain so until each makes him or herself guilty by a guilty deed. Islam does not believe in 'original sin;' and its scripture interprets Adam's disobedience as his own personal misdeed—a misdeed for which he repented and which God forgave."[5]

The Christian perspective of sin is very different. Romans 3:23 teach that "all have sinned and fall short of the glory of God." We are in a fallen state because "through one man sin entered the world, and death through sin, and so death spread to all men, because all sinned" (Rom. 5:12).

## Muslim Belief About Salvation

Islam and Christianity also have very different views about salvation that are derived from their different views of sin. Muslims often see human failings as the result of forgetfulness or as merely making mistakes. They believe that we are constantly forgetful of God, but they do not believe that we have a sin nature. Therefore, Muslims believe they can be saved by their own efforts by following the regime of the five pillars of Islam: Shahada (repetition of the creed), Salat (prayers), Zakat (almsgiving), Sawm (fast of Ramadan), and Hajj (pilgrimage to Mecca).

The Qur'an teaches that believers are to follow the straight path (Sura 1:6). Therefore they are responsible for their actions. They must do what

---

[5] Isma'il R. Al Faruqi, *Islam* (Nils, IL: Argus Communications, 1984), 9.

Allah commands in order to please him and be admitted into paradise. Obeying the five pillars of Islam is the way to achieve this reward.

Muslims do not believe they can have any assurance of their own salvation. Allah sends people to paradise or hell as he pleases: "So Allah leads astray those whom He please and guides whom He pleases and He is Exalted in power, full of wisdom" (Sura 14:4).

One image used in the Qur'an to illustrate this is the image of a scale. On the Day of Judgment, all of their works will be weighed: "Then those whose balance (of good deeds) is heavy—they will attain salvation: but those whose balance is light, will be those who have lost their souls; in hell will they abide" (Sura 23:102-103).

Apparently, even Muhammad had doubts about his own salvation. He said, "though I am the Apostle of Allah, yet I do not know what Allah will do to me" (Hadith 5:266). When Muhammad was on his night journey, he discovered good works recorded in a book: "The fate of each man. We have bound about his next. On the Day of Resurrection, We shall confront him with a book spread open, saying 'Here is your book: read it. Enough for you this day that your own soul should call you to account'" (Sura 17:13).

The question facing all Muslims is whether their good deeds will outweigh their bad deeds. Faith is certainly important, but so are good works. And since all of this is uncertain, there is no assurance of salvation.

But while salvation is unsure, damnation is certain. The Qur'an teaches that those who reject the faith (Sura 2:6, 3:32) are lost. And a Muslim believer who rejects the teachings of Islam will never be restored. That is why most Muslim parents will disown their children if they convert to Christianity. In their minds, Allah has rejected them so they must do the same.

By contrast, the biblical view of salvation is very different. The Bible teaches that Adam's sin has affected all of humanity. Romans 5:12 reads, "Therefore, just as sin entered the world through one man, and death through sin, and in this way death came to all men, because all sinned." Paul later (5:18-19) adds that "So then as through one transgression there resulted condemnation to all men, even so through one act of righteousness there resulted justification of life to all men. For as through the one man's disobedience, the many were made sinners, even so through the obedience of the One the many will be made righteous."

God is holy (Ps. 77:13), and He alone is holy (Rev. 15:4). When we try to measure our sin against God's holiness, it is impossible to balance the scales. David laments in Psalm 103:3 that "If You, Lord, should mark iniquities, O Lord, who could stand?" Another place where the Bible uses the concept of scales is in Daniel (5:27) where God's judgment falls upon Belshazzar: "You have been weighed in the balances, and found wanting." The Bible also uses the image of a measuring rod in Amos (7:7-9) to show that God's people fall short of His standard of righteousness.

The Bible clearly teaches that no one is good enough to stand before His righteousness. The Old Testament says that "all our righteous deeds are like a filthy garment" (Isaiah 64:6). The New Testament teaches that we are made righteous not by doing good works (Eph. 2:8-9) but by faith in the death of Christ on the cross. Jesus paid the penalty for sin that we might have everlasting life.

## Heaven, Hell, and Judgment

The Qur'an frequently talks about a coming "Day of Judgment." It is depicted as a time of wrath, retribution, and judgment (Sura 55). Islam teaches that the final hour will come suddenly. Natural disasters will occur, and graves will open up (Sura 75; 82; 84).

This day is often described as the day of wrath or the day of decision or the day of truth. On this day, every person will stand before Allah, and a scroll will come down accounting for all his or her deeds. "On the Day of Judgment We shall bring out for him a scroll, which he will see spread open. It will be said to him, Read thine own record. Sufficient is thy soul this day to make out an account against thee" (Sura 17:13-14).

Also on that day, their deeds will be weighed on a great scale. If it tips toward righteousness, the person will go to paradise. If not, he or she will go to hell. Allah determines your destiny: "Yea, to Allah, belongs all that is in the heavens and on earth; so that He rewards those who do evil, according to their deeds, and He rewards those who do good, with what is best" (Sura 53;31).

Paradise is a place of beauty, with streams of clear water as well as rivers of milk and fountains of honey. It is also a place of sensual and sexual delight (Sura 3:14-15; 47:15; 55).

Hell is a place of burning. Brains are boiled, and molten lead is poured into ears. The poor souls have faces covered in fire (Sura 14:50; 76:4). Hell is the place where idolaters and infidels can be found. The Hadith seems to teach that more women are in hell than men.

One Muslim tradition teaches that Jesus will return to earth as the Messiah. Supposedly he will destroy all crosses, kill all pigs, and be buried next to Muhammad when he dies. Another tradition says that a messiah figure (known as *Mahdi*) will come to earth and join with Jesus to fight against the Antichrist. He will then institute a kingdom of justice.

# SECTION 2 Islam and Terrorism

Islam is the second largest religion in the world and is the fastest growing. This has led to a clash of civilizations with the West. Why is this conflict occurring? What is sharia law and how is it being implemented in our world today? How can we fight radical Muslim terrorism overseas and even in our own country?

# CHAPTER 4 – THE CLASH OF CIVILIZATIONS

Before we look at the rise of Muslim terrorism in our world, we need to understand the worldview conflict between Islam and western values. The Muslim religion is a seventh-century religion. Think about that statement for a moment. Most people would not consider Christianity a first-century religion. While it began in the first century, it has taken the timeless message of the Bible and communicated it in contemporary ways.

In many ways, Islam is still stuck in the century in which it developed. One of the great questions is whether it will adapt to the modern world. The rise of Muslim terrorism and the desire to implement sharia law illustrate this clash of civilizations.

## The Clash of Civilizations

In the summer of 1993, Samuel Huntington published an article entitled "The Clash of Civilizations?" in the journal *Foreign Affairs*.[6] The article generated more controversy than any other article in the journal since the 1940s. And Huntington says it stirred up more debate than anything else he wrote during that time.

---

[6] Samuel P. Huntington, "The Clash of Civilizations? *Foreign Affairs*, Summer 1993, 22-49.

Three years later Samuel Huntington published a book using a similar title. *The Clash of Civilizations and the Remaking of World Order* came on the market in 1996 and became a bestseller, once again stirring controversy. It seems worthy to revisit his comments and predictions because they have turned out to be remarkably accurate.

His thesis was fairly simple. World history will be marked by conflicts between three principal groups: western universalism, Muslim militancy, and Chinese assertion.

Huntington says that in the post-Cold War world, "global politics has become multipolar and multicivilizational."[7] During most of human history, major civilizations were separated from one another and contact was intermittent or non-existent. That pattern changed in the modern era (around 1500 A.D.). For over 400 years, the nation states of the West (Britain, France, Spain, Austria, Prussia, Germany, and the United States) constituted a multipolar international system that interacted, competed, and fought wars with each other. During that same period of time, these nations also expanded, conquered, and colonized nearly every other civilization.

During the Cold War, global politics became bipolar, and the world was divided into three parts. Western democracies led by the United States engaged in ideological, political, economic, and even military competition with communist countries led

[7] Samuel P. Huntington, *The Clash of Civilizations and the Remaking of World Order* (New York: Simon & Schuster, 1996), 21.

by the Soviet Union. Much of this conflict occurred in the Third World outside these two camps and was composed mostly of non-aligned nations.

Huntington argued that in the post-Cold War world, the principal actors are still the nation states, but they are influenced by more than just power and wealth. Other factors like cultural preferences, commonalities, and differences are also influential. The most important groupings are not the three blocs of the Cold War, but rather the major world civilizations. Most significant in our discussion is the conflict between the Western world and Muslim militancy.

Bernard Lewis sees this conflict as a phase the Islam is currently experiencing in which many Muslim leaders are attempting to resist the influences of the modern world (and in particular the Western world) on their communities and countries. This is what he had to say about Islam and the modern world:

> Islam has brought comfort and peace of mind to countless millions of men and women. It has given dignity and meaning to drab and impoverished lives. It has taught people of different races to live in brotherhood and people of different creeds to live side by side in reasonable tolerance. It inspired a great civilization in which others besides Muslims lived creative and useful lives and which, by its achievement, enriched the whole world. But Islam, like other religions, has also known periods when it inspired in some of its followers a

mood of hatred and violence. It is our misfortune that part, though by no means all or even most, of the Muslim world is now going through such a period, and that much, though again not all, of that hatred is directed against us.[8]

This does not mean that all Muslims want to engage in jihad warfare against America and the West. But it does mean that there is a growing clash of civilizations. Muslims see the world divided into two camps, and this view intensifies the clash between the West and Islam. Bernard Lewis explains:

In the classical Islamic view, to which many Muslims are beginning to return, the world and all mankind are divided into two: the House of Islam, where the Muslim law and faith prevail, and the rest, known as the House of Unbelief or the House of War, which it is the duty of Muslims ultimately to bring to Islam. It should by now be clear that we are facing a mood and a movement far transcending the level of issues and policies and the governments that pursue them. This is no less than a clash of civilizations—the perhaps irrational but surely historic reaction of an ancient rival against our Judeo-Christian heritage, our secular present, and the worldwide expansion of both. It is crucially important that we on our side should not be provoked

---

[8] Bernard Lewis, The Roots of Muslim Rage," *Atlantic Monthly*, September 1990, www.theatlantic.com/doc/prem/199009/muslim-rage.

into an equally historic but also equally irrational reaction against the rival.[9]

Not everyone accepts the analysis of Samuel Huntington regarding conflict between Western democracies and Muslim militancy. For example, William Tucker believes that the actual conflict results from what he calls the Muslim intelligentsia. He says "that we are not facing a clash of civilizations so much as a conflict with an educated segment of a civilization that produces some very weird, sexually disoriented men. Poverty has nothing to do with it. It is stunning to meet the al Qaeda roster—one highly accomplished scholar after another with advanced degrees in chemistry, biology, medicine, engineering, a large percentage of them educated in the United States."[10]

His analysis is contrary to the many statements that have been made in the past that poverty breeds terrorism. While it is certainly true that many recruits for jihad come from impoverished situations, it is also true that the leadership comes from those who are well-educated and highly accomplished.

William Tucker believes that those who wish to engage in jihad warfare against the US and the West bear a striking resemblance to the student revolutionaries during the 1960s on American universities. He calls them "overprivileged children" who he believes need to prove themselves (and their

---

[9] Ibid.

[10] William Tucker, "Overprivileged Children," *American Spectator*, 12 Sept. 2006, www.spectator.org/dsp_article.asp?art_id=10342.

manhood) in the world. He also believes that "this is confounded by a polygamous society where fathers are often distant from their sons and where men and women barely encounter each other as young adults."

Tucker, therefore, concludes that we are effectively at war with a Muslim intelligentsia. These are essentially "the same people who brought us the horrors of the French Revolution and 20th century Communism. With their obsession for moral purity and their rational hatred that goes beyond all irrationality, these warrior-intellectuals are wreaking the same havoc in the Middle East as they did in Jacobin France and Mao Tse-tung's China."

One of the most watched Internet video debates on Islam involved Wafa Sultan, who debated Al-Jazeera host Faisal al-Qasim and Islamic scholar Ibrahim Al-Khouli about Samuel P. Huntington's idea of a "clash of civilizations." The exchange took place on the 90-minute discussion program "The Opposite Direction," with Sultan speaking via satellite from Los Angeles.[11] Here are two excerpts of what she said:

The clash we are witnessing around the world is not a clash of religions or a clash of civilizations," she said. "It is a clash between two opposites, between two eras. It is a clash between a mentality that belongs to the Middle Ages and another mentality that belongs to the 21st century. It is a clash between

---

[11] The video clip from Al-Jazeera television that was seen on the Internet was produced by the Middle East Media Research Institute: http://switch5.castup.net/frames/20041020_MemriTV_Popup/video_48 0x360.asp?ai=214&ar=1050wmv&ak=null.

civilization and backwardness, between the civilized and the primitive, between barbarity and rationality. It is a clash between freedom and oppression, between democracy and dictatorship. It is a clash between human rights, on the one hand, and the violation of these rights, on the other hand. It is a clash between those who treat women like beasts and those who treat them like human beings. What we see today is not a clash of civilizations. Civilizations do not clash but compete.

The Muslims are the ones who began using this expression. The Muslims are the ones who began the clash of civilizations. The Prophet of Islam said: 'I was ordered to fight the people until they believe in Allah and His Messenger.' When the Muslims divided the people into Muslims and non-Muslims and called to fight the others until they believe in what they themselves believe, they started this clash, and began this war. In order to stop this war, they must re-examine their Islamic books and curricula, which are full of calls for takfir and fighting the infidels.

## Threat from Radical Islam

It is hard to estimate the extent of this threat, but there are some commentators who have tried to provide a reasonable estimate. Dennis Prager provides an overview of the extent of the threat:

> Anyone else sees the contemporary reality—the genocidal Islamic regime in Sudan; the widespread Muslim theological and emotional support for the killing of a Muslim who converts to another religion;

the absence of freedom in Muslim-majority countries; the widespread support for Palestinians who randomly murder Israelis; the primitive state in which women are kept in many Muslim countries; the celebration of death; the honor killings of daughters, and so much else that is terrible in significant parts of the Muslim world—knows that civilized humanity has a new evil to fight.[12]

He argues that just as previous generations had to fight the Nazis and the communists, so this generation has to confront militant Islam. But he also notes something is dramatically different about the present Muslim threat. He says:

Far fewer people believed in Nazism or in communism than believe in Islam generally or in authoritarian Islam specifically. There are one billion Muslims in the world. If just 10 percent believe in the Islam of Hamas, the Taliban, the Sudanese regime, Saudi Arabia, Wahhabism, bin Laden, Islamic Jihad, the Finley Park Mosque in London or Hizbollah—and it is inconceivable that only one of 10 Muslims supports any of these groups' ideologies— that means a true believing enemy of at least 100 million people.[13]

---

[12] Dennis Prager, "The Islamic Threat is Greater than German and Soviets Threats Were," 29 May 2006, www.townhall.com/columnists/DennisPrager/2006/03/28/the_islamic_t hreat_is_greater_than_german_and_soviet_threats_were.

[13] Ibid.

This very large number of people who wish to destroy civilization poses a threat that is unprecedented. Never has civilization has to confront such large numbers of those would wish to destroy civilization.

So, what is the threat in the United States? Let's take one number and one percentage for an estimate. There are about 4 million Muslim-Americans in the U.S., and we are often told that nearly all are law-abiding citizens. So let's assume that percentage is even as high as 99 percent. That still leaves one percent who believe in jihad and could pose a threat to America. Multiply one percent by 4 million, and you get a number of 40,000 individuals that Homeland Security needs to try to monitor. Even if you use a percentage of one-tenth of one percent, you still get about 4,000 potential terrorists in America.

## Islamic Tipping Point

When the Muslim population increases in a country, there are certain social changes that have been documented. Peter Hammond deals with this in his book, *Slavery Terrorism, & Islam*. Most people have never read the book, but many have seen an email on one of the most quoted parts of the book.[14]

He argued that when the Muslim population is under five percent, the primary activity is proselytizing, usually from ethnic minorities and the disaffected. By the time the Muslim population

[14] Peter Hammond, *Slavery Terrorism, & Islam: The Historical Roots and Contemporary Threat* (San Jose, CA: Frontline, 1982), 151.

reaches five percent or more, it begins to exert its influence and start pushing for sharia law.

Peter Hammond sees a significant change when a Muslim population reaches ten percent (found in many European countries). At that point, he says you begin to see increased levels of violence and lawlessness. You also begin to hear statements of identity and the filing of various grievances.

At twenty to thirty percent, there are examples of hair-trigger rioting and jihad militias. In some countries, you even have church bombings. By forty percent to fifty percent, nations like Bosnia and Lebanon experience widespread massacres and ongoing militia warfare. When at least half the population is Muslim, you begin to see the country persecute infidels and apostates and Sharia law is implemented over all of its citizens.

After eighty percent, you see countries like Iran, Syria, and Nigeria engage in persecution and intimidation as a daily part of life. Sometimes state-run genocide develops in an attempt to purge the country of all infidels. The final goal is "Dar-es-Salaam" (the Islamic House of Peace).

Peter Hammond would probably be the first to say that these are generalizations and there are certainly exceptions to the rule. But the general trends have been validated through history. When the Muslim population is small, it leaders focus on winning converts and working to gain sympathy for sharia law. But then their numbers increase, the radical Muslims leaders take over, and the Islamic domination begins.

# Christian Implications of the Clash of Civilizations

This clash of civilizations has a profound impact on missions. In the past, countries that were closed to the gospel tended to be communist countries. Even so, there was still a significant amount of Christian growth in countries behind the Iron Curtain and Bamboo Curtain. With the collapse of the Soviet Union, many of these countries are more open to the gospel than ever before. Meanwhile, persecution of Christians remains in China.

But a new phenomenon has emerged. Muslim countries are now the most resistant to the message of Christianity. Mission work is limited or even non-existent in many of these Muslim countries. This represents the greatest challenge for missions in the 21st century: reaching the Muslim world for Christ. Already there are over a billion and a half Muslims in the world, making Islam the second largest religion in the world and one of the fastest growing.

A second implication is related to the first. Samuel Huntington predicts a growing conflict between western universalism and Muslim militancy. In other words, the conflict is between liberal western democracies and their cultures and Muslim countries.

This presents a major challenge for Christians trying to reach Muslims. When they see the West with its immorality and decadence, they reject it and Christianity. After all, they reason, these are Christian countries, and this is what they produce.

It is crucial for Christians to make a distinction between Christianity and western society. The political conflict may be between western democracies and Muslim militancy, but the spiritual battle is between Christianity and Islam. The two are not the same.

## Reforming Islam

Will this clash of civilizations continue, or is it possible to reform Islam so that it finds a peaceful place in the modern world? One book that attempts to explain the challenge that Islam faces in the modern world is the book, *Inside the Revolution*, Joel Rosenberg explains the challenge Islam faces in the modern world. He discussed the three most dramatic movements of our time.[15]

The first is what he calls "the Radicals." These are radical Muslims who want to annihilate the United States and Israel. Many of them in Iran believe the Islamic Messiah's arrival on Earth is "imminent" and the End of Days is at hand. The book and documentary talk about the potential danger of these Muslims acquiring nuclear weapons so they might achieve their apocalyptic objectives.

The second group is "the Reformers." These Muslims believe that that the Radicals are wrong. The book and his DVD documentary talk about the hope that these Reformers can create real democracies in the Middle East.

---

[15] Joel Rosenberg, *Inside the Revolution: How the Followers of Jihad, Jefferson, and Jesus Are Battling to Dominate the Middle East and Transform the World* (Carol Stream, IL: Tyndale House, 2009).

The third group is "the Revivalists." Millions of Muslims are abandoning Islam and turning to faith in Jesus Christ. The book and documentary explain how this is happening. These are fascinating stories.

The subtitle of the book, *Inside the Revolution*, tells it all. It says: "How the followers of Jihad, Jefferson, and Jesus are battling to dominate the Middle East and transform the world." These are the three groups within Islam that will be influential in this century: the Radicals, the Reformers, and the Revivalists.

Changes in Islam will have to come from within (the Reformers) and perhaps also from without (the Revivalists). This leads to one of the most asked questions when there is a terrorist attack. Where are the modern Muslims? Where are the voices from these potential reformers?

Christine Douglass-Williams tried to answer that question in her book, *The Challenge of Modernizing Islam*.[16] It includes interviews with many of these moderate Muslims trying to bring reform. Early on in the book, she says the original title talked about reforming Islam. She and the publisher concluded that wasn't precise enough. She points out that currently there is a turf war within Islam "between those who seek to reform Islam back to the seventh century and those who seek to reform it to modernity."

The first part of her book includes interviews she has done with moderate Muslims like Dr. Zudhi

[16] Christine Douglass-Williams, *The Challenge of Modernizing Islam* (NY: Encounter, 2017).

Jasser, Dr. Tawfik Hamid, and Raheel Raza. We don't hear about them in the mainstream media too often because many of them aren't provided a platform. We also have to acknowledge that many of them are threatened if they speak out. The subtitle of Christine Douglass-Williams book says it all: "Reformers Speak Out and the Obstacles They Face."

It is also worth mentioning that not all moderates are reformers. Reformers usually insist that the texts in Islam must be subject to new interpretations. To do so will be difficult. It might mean having to set aside fourteen centuries of interpretation as well as Muslim history.

One illustration can be found in the writings of Tawfik Hamid who countered the common belief that Islam has been a religion of peace. He explained that the approved Islamic literature "teaches violent principles such a killing apostates, beating women, killing gays, and enslaving female war prisoners for sexual purposes."

He went on to say that if you want to disprove what he said, all you would have to do is provide texts that have been "accepted by the leading Islamic scholars at Al-Azhar University or the religious authorities in Saudi Arabia." These religious bodies are the ones responsible for approving a printed Qur'an.

All the critics would have to do is "produce a solitary approved Islamic text that stands clearly and unambiguously against, for example, killing apostates, beating women, killing gays, and enslaving female war prisoners for the express purpose of raping them." He says they won't be able to produce such a text because it does not exist.[17]

[17] Tawfik Hamid, "Carson Is Right About Muslims," *Newsmax*, 23 September 2015, www.newsmax.com/TawfikHamid/Ben-Carson-Middle-East-Religion/2015/09/23/id/692925/.

# CHAPTER 5 - SHARIA LAW

People living in the Western world generally accept the concept of a true separation of the institutions of church and state. Hundreds of years of Western tradition have demonstrated the wisdom of keeping these institutions separated and the danger that ensues when the ecclesiastical and civil institutions are melded into one.

That is not the case with Muslims, especially in other countries. A recent Pew Research poll found that 99 percent of Muslims in Afghanistan, 91 percent of Muslims in Iraq and 84 percent in Pakistan favor making sharia the official law of their country. [18]

## Sharia Law

A foundational practice of Islam is the implementation of *sharia* into the legal structure. The term *sharia* is derived from the verb *shara'a*. Sharia is a system of divine law, belief, or practice that is based upon Muslim legal interpretation. It applies to economics, politics, and society. Most Muslims distinguish between *fiqh* (which deals with the details of Islam) and *sharia* (which refers to the principles behind those details). Ideally, both should be in harmony with each other.

---

[18] Michael Lipka, "Muslims and Islam: Key Findings in the U.S. and Around the World," *Pew Research*, 9 August, 2017, www.pewresearch.org/fact-tank/2017/08/09/muslims-and-islam-key-findings-in-the-u-s-and-around-the-world/

Sometimes the world has been able to see how extreme the interpretation of *sharia* can be. Muslims have been put to death when they have been accused of adultery or homosexuality. They have been put to death for leaving the religion of Islam. And these are not isolated examples.

A number of years ago, Pew research asked Muslims very specific questions about how far they would implement sharia law. The survey found that 89 percent of Muslims in Pakistan, 85 percent of Muslims in Afghanistan, and 84 percent of Muslims in Egypt favor stoning as a punishment for adultery. The survey also found that 86 percent of Muslims in Egypt and 82 percent of Muslims in Jordan favor the death penalty for any Muslim who leaves the religion of Islam.[19]

## Jews and Christians Under Sharia Law

It should not be surprising that Christians are persecuted in Muslim countries. Each year, the organization Open Doors publishes its World Watch List that identifies where Christians are persecuted. Over the last few years, nine of the top ten countries that that practice extreme persecution of Christians is Muslim countries.[20]

Treating Jews and Christians under sharia law is justified in the Qur'an. For example, the Qur'an talks

---

[19] "Beliefs About Sharia," *Pew Research Center*, 30 April 2013, http://www.pewforum.org/2013/04/30/the-worlds-muslims-religion-politics-society-beliefs-about-sharia/

[20] Open Doors, "Christian Persecution-World Watch List – 2017, https://www.opendoorsusa.org/christian-persecution/world-watch-list/

about "people of the book." Sura 9:29 says, "Fight those who believe not in Allah nor the Last Day, nor hold that forbidden which hath been forbidden by Allah and His Prophet, nor acknowledge the religion of Truth, (even if they are) of the People of the Book, until they pay the jizyah with willing submission, and feel themselves subdued."

The "people of the book" (*Ahl al-Kitab*) refers to Jews and Christians. Islamic law refers to them as *dhimmis.* They have protected status and were to live as "protected people: (*Ahl al-dhimma*). But they had to live as second-class citizens in a Muslim state.

Muhammad made a distinction between infidels, who were pagans and polytheists, and the "people of the book," who had received revelations from the prophets (Moses, Jesus). The latter group is protected in one sense because they have received these revelations. But they are also guilty because (according to Islam) they have distorted these teachings and rejected the teaching of Muhammad. Although this status was originally given only to the "people of the book," it was later extended to other religions (Sikhs, Zoroastrians, etc.).

Because of their guilt, Islamic teaching stipulates that Jews and Christians may live in a Muslim country, but not as equals to other Muslims. Usually, this means that they may not participate in the government. They may practice their religion, but with many restrictions. For example, they were not allowed to have any external manifestations of worship (procession with the cross, ringing bells).

These restrictions are another part of the verse that requires the *dhimmis* must "feel themselves subdued." In the past, they has meant: (1) that they could not prevent a fellow Christian from converting to Islam, (2) that they could not erect a cross on their church building, and (3) that they must dress in a certain way that would identify them as Jews or Christians.

Finally, they must pay the *jizya*, which is the poll tax required from every *dhimmi*. In earlier times, this was a major source of income for the Muslim government from dhimmi who paid both the personal tax and the land tax.

The Qur'an teaches (2:256) that, "there is no compulsion in religion." But is that really so? It depends on your definition of compulsion. A closer look at Islamic law demonstrates a veiled threat that many believe in tantamount to compulsion. For example, Muhammad instructed his followers to invite non-Muslims to accept Islam before waging war against them. If they refused, warfare would follow or second class status. They would be inferiors in the Muslim social order and pay the *jizya* as required in Sura 9:29. If they pay it, they may live, but if they refuse to pay it, warfare will ensue.

## Christians Treatment Within Islam

After its rapid expansion in the seventh-century, Islam developed a practice of allowing Jews and Christian to live within their society but with many restrictions. The Pact of Umar set forth twenty-eight limitations on their rights and practices.[21] For example, Christians:

• "shall not build, in our cities build, in our cities or in their neighborhood, new monasteries, churches, convents, or monks' cells, nor shall we repair, by day or by night, such of them as fall in ruins or are situated in the quarters of the Muslims."

• "shall not manifest our religion publicly nor convert anyone to it."

• "shall not prevent any of our kin from entering Islam if they wish it."

• "shall not display our crosses or our books in the roads or markets of the Muslims" and "shall only use clappers in our churches very softly."

• "shall not raise our voices in our church services or in the presence of Muslims nor shall we raise our voices when following our dead."

In modern times, the application of dimmitude varies from country to country. In many Muslim countries today, non-Muslims must pay the *jizya* and must wear a wide cloth belt, known as the *zunnar* to identify them. Sometimes they must keep to the side of the street. And they are never greeted with the traditional Muslim greeting "as-Salamu 'alaykum' (which means "Peace be with you").[22]

In many cases, non-Muslims are persecuted and killed. A number of excellent books document the way in which Christians have been persecuted in

---

[21] Pact of Umar, http://en.wikipedia.org/wiki/Pact_of_Umar.

[22] Umdat al-Salik (*Reliance of the Traveller*), o11.3-5.

Muslim countries.[23] For example, between 1905 and 1918, Ottoman Turks killed over two million Armenian Christians. Since Muslims came to power in Sudan and declared jihad on Christians, there have been more than three million killed.

Sharia Law and Apostates

It is difficult for a Muslim to leave the faith of Islam. A Muslim is considered part of a larger community of Muslim believers. He or she is a member of the *umma*, which is an Arabic word meaning community or nation.

When a Muslim decides to leave the faith, there are repercussions in the family and community. The family is embarrassed and will even lose respect within the Muslim community. The mosque feels it has failed in its duty and lost a member to ignorance and idolatry.

The Qur'an teaches that an apostate Muslim faces the wrath of Allah (Sura 47:25-28). Sharia law in many countries treats apostasy as the unforgivable sin and therefore punishable by death. Often, they are referred to as *kafir*, which is the Arabic word for the unbeliever. It applies to those who reject the teachings of Islam and the Qur'an.

Many Muslim countries have laws against apostasy. Islam teaches that once you are a Muslim,

---

[23] Paul Marshall, *Their Blood Cries Out: The Worldwide Tragedy of Modern Christians Who Are Dying for their Faith* (Dallas: Word, 1997) and Emir Fethi Caner and H. Edward Pruit, *The Costly Call: Modern-Day Stories of Muslims Who Found Jesus* (Grand Rapids, MI: Kregel, 2005).

you are always a Muslim. Leaving the Muslim faith can have harsh consequences, including death.

## Sharia Law and Women

There is great confusion about the status of women within Islam. Some Muslim leaders claim that Islam actually liberates women. One Muslim women's advocate actually said that the "Islamic religion has given women more rights than any other religion has, and has guaranteed her honour and pride."[24] That might surprise the women who lived under the rule of the Taliban in Afghanistan or who live under Sharia law in many Muslims countries today.

While it is true that many Muslims no doubt do respect and honor women, it is not true that those ideas can be found in the Qur'an. Here are just a few passages that illustrate the way women are to be treated.

• According to the Qur'an women are considered inferior to men: "Men have authority over women because God has made the one superior to the other" (Sura 4:34).

• The Qur'an restricts a woman's testimony in court. Her testimony is worth half as much as that of a man (Sura 2:282).

---

[24] Nawal El-Saadawi, quoted in *The Ideal Muslimah: The True Islamic Personality of the Muslim Woman as Defined in the Qur'an and Sunnah*, www.usc.edu/dept/MSA/humanrelations/womeninislam/idealmuslimah/ .

• The Qur'an teaches that a son's inheritance should be twice that of a daughter's: "Allah thus directs you as regards your children's inheritance; to the male, a portion equal to that of two females" (Sura 4:11).

• Islam sanctions polygamy (with up to four wives) as well as sex with slave women: "If we fear that ye shall not be able to deal justly with the orphans, marry women of your choice, two or three or four; but if we fear that ye shall not be able to deal justly with them, then only one, or a captive that your hand possess, that will be more suitable, to prevent you from doing injustice" (Sura 4:3)

• Wives are subject to their husbands. If wives are disloyal or disobedient, the Qur'an sets forth their punishment. The husband is first to admonish them, then not sleep with them, and third to beat them lightly. Essentially, wives are subject to the control of their husbands (Sura 2:223; 4:34).

## Sharia Law and Polygamy

In Arabia before the time of Muhammad, polygamy was common. A man could have as many wives as he could support. The Qur'an instructed a man to have two, three, or four wives. However, Muhammad had a special revelation that allowed him to have more than four wives. The Qur'an also taught that he could marry prisoners of war, daughters of uncles and aunts, and any believing woman (Sura 33:50).

Even though the Qur'an allows for polygamy, many nations prohibit multiple wives. Turkey, for example, banned polygamy in 1926. Islamic law allows a Muslim man to marry a non-Muslim woman. However, a Muslim woman may only marry a Muslim man.

There is also the concept of Mut'a which has developed in Islam that allows a Muslim man to take a temporary "wife" for a sexual relationship. This may be done when he is in military service, although it has also been abused in justifying prostitution in which a Muslim man takes a prostitute as a temporary "wife" for the night.

## Sharia Law and Rights of Women

Sometimes women participate in public prayer in mosques, other times they do not. A formal prayer in public in the mosque is a public demonstration of a Muslim's faith. But women's participation varies according to culture and time period.

The formal times of prayer are attended by the men. If women are allowed to attend, they are segregated and wear their veils.

The veiling and seclusion of women have been part of the Muslim culture since the beginnings of Islam. In the Qur'an, Muhammad commands his wives and daughters to draw veils around them. This has been applied to all Muslim women. The veil would allow them to be recognized but not molested (Sura 33:59).

The Qur'an teaches that women must "lower their gaze and guard their modesty: that they should not display their beauty and ornaments except what must ordinarily appear thereof: that they should draw their veils over their bosoms and not display their beauty except to their husbands, their fathers" (Sura 24:31).

The veils actually do more than just cover the face and body of women. The veil establishes the significant distinction between men and women. The veil separates women from men and from public life.

Women cover themselves in different ways and in different cultures, ranging from burkas to scarves. Sometimes the command for women to cover themselves has had tragic consequences. In March 2002, fifteen girls died in a fire in Saudi Arabia. Since there were no men in the school, the girls took off their Islamic garb for the lesson. When a fire broke out in the building, they tried to escape but were stopped by the Saudi religious police, (known as the *Muttawa*). They would not allow them to leave the building because they were not veiled. They apparently reasoned that death for the girls was preferable to the risk of subjecting men in the vicinity to impure thoughts.

Islamic law states that a "husband may forbid his wife to leave the home."[25] It also states, "a woman may not leave the city without her husband or a member of her unmarriageable kin accompanying her, unless the journey is obligatory, like the hajj. It is unlawful for her to travel otherwise, and unlawful for her husband to allow her to."[26]

---

[25] "Umdat al-Salik, (manual of Islamic law), m 10.4

[26] Ibid., m 10.3

These laws were practiced in Afghanistan under the Taliban and are observed in countries like Saudi Arabia. In that country, women cannot drive nor can they leave their home without being accompanied by a male family member. Amnesty International reports that women in Saudi Arabia "who walk unaccompanied or are in the company of a man who is neither their husband nor close relative, are at risk of arrest on suspicion of prostitution" or other moral offenses.[27]

Divorce is relatively easy in Islam. All a husband needs to do is say to his wife, "I divorce you." The divorce is final at that moment. The Qur'an does, however, provide a mechanism for resolving disputes: "If a wife fears cruelty or desertion on her husband's part, there is no blame on them if they arrange an amicable settlement between themselves; and such settlements is best" (Sura 4:128).

The Qur'an also instructs men to follow a waiting period to make sure their divorced wife is not pregnant: "if you divorce your wives, divorce them at the end of their waiting period" (Sura 65:1). In reality, though, a woman can be put out of the house in minutes and divorced.

One passage in the Qur'an seems to provide justification for child marriage. The following verses say, "the same shall apply to those who have not yet menstruated" (Sura 65:4). So the passage seems to consider the possibility that a man may be married to a girl who has not even reached adolescence.

---

[27] Amnesty International, "Saudi Arabia: End Secrecy End Suffering: Women," www.amnesty.org/ailib/intcam/saudi/briefing/4.html.

Child marriages were common in the Arab peninsula during the time in which the Qur'an was written. One of Muhammad's wives was a child bride of six and he apparently consummated the marriage when she was nine years old.

Such marriages are still common in some Muslim countries today. It is estimated that half the teenage girls in some countries (such as Afghanistan) are married.[28] Iranian girls can get married when they are as young as nine with parental permission, or thirteen without consent.[29]

We have already noted that a woman's testimony in a court of law is equal to half of a man's testimony. When it comes to an accusation of rape, there must be four adult males of "impeccable" character in order to confirm a woman's accusation of rape. In fact, they must see the act itself (e.g., must witness the penetration).

This stringent requirement was based upon the incident in Muhammad's life involving Aisha who was accused of infidelity. Muhammad proclaimed her innocence, and at the same time instituted this legal requirement for sexual sins. Muhammad asked, "Why did they not produce four witnesses? Since they produce not witnesses, they verily are liars in the sight of Allah" (Sura 24:13).

Because of this legal requirement, it is nearly impossible to prove rape in Muslim countries

---

[28] United Nations Children's Fund, "UNICEF: Child marriages must stop," 7 March 2001, www.unicef.org/newsline/01pr21.htm.

[29] Lisa Beyer, "The Women of Islam," Time, 25 Nov. 2001.

governed by Sharia law. Essentially, men can commit rape with impunity. Unless she can produce four credible male witnesses, the perpetrator goes free.

But the injustice doesn't end there. Often the rape victim's charge of rape is used in court as an admission of adultery. So, while the rapist goes free, often she is incarcerated. It has been estimated that in Pakistan as many as 75 percent of the women in prison are there because they were victims of rape.[30]

## Sharia Law and the Constitution

Sharia law is very different in many respects from the laws established through the U.S. Constitution and the laws established through English Common law. In an attempt to prevent sharia law from being implemented in America, a number of state legislatures (Alabama, Arizona, Kansas, Louisiana, North Carolina, South Dakota, and Tennessee) have such bans on sharia law. Voters in other states have approved a ban that has been struck down by a federal appeals court.

Although opponents argue that these sharia law bans are unnecessary, various studies have found significant cases of sharia law being allowed in U.S. court. One report with the title, "Shariah Law and the American State Courts"[31] found 50 significant

---

[30] Sisters in Islam, "Rape, Zina, and Incest," 6 April 2000, www.muslimtents.com/sistersinislam/resources/sdefini.htm.

[31] Shariah law and the American State Courts, Center for Security Policy, 5 January2015. https://www.centerforsecuritypolicy.org/2015/01/05/shariah-in-american-courts-the-expanding-incursion-of-islamic-law-in-the-u-s-legal-system/.

cases of Sharia law in U.S. courts just from their small sample of appellate published cases. When they looked at state courts, they found an additional 15 cases in the trial courts and 12 more in the appellate courts. Judges are making decisions deferring to Sharia law even when those decisions conflict with the U.S. Constitution and the various state constitutions.

How should we respond to the increased use of Sharia law in America? One simple way to explain your concern to legislators, family, friends, and neighbors are to remember the numbers 1-8-14. These three numbers stand for the three amendments to the U.S. Constitution that prevent the use of Sharia law.

The First Amendment says that there should be no establishment of religion. Sharia law is based on one religion's interpretation of rights. The First Amendment prohibits the establishment of any national religion (including Islam).

The Eighth Amendment prohibits "cruel and unusual punishment." Most Americans would consider the penalties handed down under Sharia law to be cruel and unusual.

The Fourteenth Amendment guarantees each citizen equal protection under the Constitution. Sharia law does not treat men and women equally, nor does it treat Muslims and non-Muslims equally. This also violates the Constitution.

---

# CHAPTER 6 – ISLAM AND TERRORISM

Muslim terrorism has become part of our world today. That is not to say that all Muslims are terrorists. Very few Muslims even sympathize with terrorist attacks by other radical Muslims. But even if few Muslims are terrorists, it is also true that most terrorists are Muslims.

Terrorism can be defined as the use of fear and violence against innocent citizens in an attempt to strike terror and influence public opinion and public policy. The focus of terrorism is often on noncombatants in an effort to create fear. That is why many military strategists refer to terrorism as the "new warfare." Terrorists, however, turn the notion of war on its head. Innocent non-combatants become the target of terrorist attacks. Terrorist warfare holds innocent people hostage and makes a soldier and civilian alike potential targets for their aggression.

## History of Terrorism

In the past, various dictators and governments used terrorist tactics against their people or other enemies. For example, the Reign of Terror in eighteenth century France led to the execution of 25,000 people. Also, Marxist leaders used terror against its citizens in order to bring about desired political and economic changes within their countries. But terrorism changed after World War II and began to be used by revolutionary groups.

Today, nearly all the terrorist actions come from radical groups within Islam.

Whole books have been written about the history of terrorism, but a book that has a good summary of radical Muslim terrorism in our time is *The ISIS Crisis*, written by Charles Dyer and Mark Tobey.[32] Back in the 1970s, Russia invaded Afghanistan. Those fighting Russia were the Mujahideen. In an unofficial way, the United States supported them. One of the leaders was Osama bin Laden. When Russia left, the Taliban filled the vacuum created when Soviet domination ended. The word *Taliban* means "students" in Pashto. This was a name given to it because many of the original members studied a radical form of Islam that was taught in Pakistani religious schools called madrassas.

When Mohammed Omar seized power, this allowed Osama bin Laden back into the country to build al Qaeda and set up terrorist training camps. The word *al Queda* means "the base." This base of operations allowed them to carry out various attacks in Saudi Arabia, Kenya, and Tanzania. One of those attacks came against the United States on September 11, 2001.

When the United States and other western powers sent troops first to Afghanistan and then Iraq, al Qaeda decentralized and became a franchise operation. The leader in Iraq was a man by the name Abu Musab al-Zarqawi. When he was killed, ISIS (now often called the Islamic State) filled that power

---

[32] Charles Dyer and Mark Tobey, *The ISIS Crisis* (Chicago, Moody, 2015), 31-44.

vacuum. Abu Bakr al-Baghdadi became the head of the Islamic State of Iraq. This was happening during the so-called "Arab Spring." Over time ISIS became the richest terrorist group in the world and controlled territory as large as an entire nation-state.

## Terrorist Interpretation of the Qur'an

Radical Muslim terrorists interpret the Qur'an literally and believe that the various verses of the sword apply to them today. Here are just a few of the verses that can justify jihad against unbelievers and infidels that are found in one chapter of the Qur'an:

• Sura 9:5 – "Fight and slay the pagans wherever you find them, and seize them, beleager them, and lie in wait for them in every stratagem."

• Sura 9:29 – "Fight those who believe not in Allah nor the Last Day, nor hold that forbidden which hath been forbidden by Allah and His Prophet, nor acknowledge the religion of Truth, (even if they are) of the People of the Book, until they pay the jizyah with willing submission, and feel themselves subdued."

• Sura 9:73 - "Strive hard against the unbelievers and the hypocrites, and be firm against them. Their abode is Hell, and evil refuge indeed."

The word translated "strive hard" is the Arabic word jahidi, which is a verbal form of the noun jihad. The traditional interpretation was that this striving was to be on the battlefield.

Muslims often divide the Qur'an into two parts: the "Meccan" and "Medinan" suras. The Meccan suras come from Muhammad's career as a prophet. In Medina, his positions hardened and are filled with matters of law and ritual. This includes exhortations to jihad.

Many Muslims remind us that there are many verses in the Qur'an that talk about peace and tolerance. That is true, but they date from the Meccan period when Muhammad was a prophet. Radical Muslim terrorists instead point to the verses written when Muhammad was in Medina. They also use the Islamic doctrine of abrogation, which means that Allah can change or cancel what he tells Muslims (Sura 2:106). They argue that these later verses abrogate (or invalidate) the earlier verses and thus are normative today.

## Western Denial of Terrorism

Radical Muslim terrorists cite the Qur'an as their justification. Nevertheless, many political and religious leaders in the west continue to argue that jihadists are not Muslims.

After the attack on Charlie Hedbo in Paris, former Vermont Governor Howard Dean said, "I stopped calling these people Muslim terrorists. They're about as Muslim as I am. I mean, they have no respect for anybody else's life, that's not what the Koran says. Europe has an enormous radical problem. I think ISIS is a cult. Not an Islamic cult. I think it's a cult."[33]

In a recent address on Muslim terrorism, the Pope argued that, "Christian terrorism does not exist, Jewish terrorism does not exist, and Muslim terrorism does not exist."[34] If the pontiff's observation was to say that not all Christians and not all Muslims are terrorists, that is obvious. It is a self-evident fact.

The problem with these and many other comments is that they attempt to distinguish radical Muslim terrorists from peace-loving Muslims by saying that the former aren't Muslims while the latter are Muslims. But these jihadists actually point to the life of Muhammad to justify their terrorist actions and they cite verses in the Qur'an that they believe justify their terrorist actions.

Our world today does not have to deal with Christian terrorists or Jewish terrorists. Even if they existed, there are appropriate verses in the Bible (1 Samuel 24:4-13; Proverbs 25:21-22; Matthew 5:41-48; Luke 6:27-32, 10:29-37: Romans 12:14-21) that can be used to condemn terrorist acts.

In an article in *The Atlantic* Graeme Wood explains who ISIS and the Islamic State are. He says "that the Islamic State is Islamic. Very Islamic. Yes, it

---

[33] Howard Dean on MSNBC's "Morning Joe," 7 January 2015, https://www.realclearpolitics.com/video/2015/01/07/howard_dean_on _paris_attack_i_stopped_calling_these_people_muslim_terrorists.html.

[34] Thomas Williams, "Pope Francis: Muslim Terrorism Does Not Exist, *Breitbart*, 17 February 2017,

http://www.breitbart.com/national-security/2017/02/17/pope-francis-muslim-terrorism-not-exist/

has attracted psychopaths and adventure seekers, drawn largely from the disaffected populations of the Middle East and Europe. But the religion preached by its most ardent followers derives from coherent and even learned interpretations of Islam."[35]

He goes on to add that: "Muslims can reject the Islamic State; nearly all do. But pretending that it isn't actually a religious, millenarian group, with theology that must be understood to be combatted, has already led the United States to underestimate it and back foolish schemes to counter it."

David French in a recent commentary made this arresting statement: "A series of Muslim immigrants and "visitors" are responsible for killing more Americans on American soil than the combined militaries of Imperial Japan and Nazi Germany."[36]

He reminds us that although Muslims in America make up a small fraction of the population, a very few within this religion are responsible for more terror deaths than any other group. This is an important fact to keep in mind when someone in government proposes that additional scrutiny be given to Muslims who wish to immigrate to this country. We implemented such tests and scrutiny

---

[35] Graeme Wood, "What ISIS Really Wants," *The Atlantic*, March 2015,

www.theatlantic.com/magazine/archive/2015/03/what-isis-really-wants/384980/.

[36] David French, "It's Time We Faced the Facts about the Muslim World," *National Review*, 19 September 2016, www.nationalreview.com/article/440175/chelsea-bombing-minnesota-stabbing-jihadist-threat-america-grows.

during the Cold War because of a national security threat.

### Vast Majority Myth

When a discussion turns to Muslim terrorism, people remind us that the vast majority of Muslims are peaceful and reject violence. Since we hear this comment so often, it is worth examining in more detail.

First, it is not necessarily true that most Muslims in other countries are peaceful and reject violence. The Pew Research polls cited earlier illustrate that the vast majorities of Muslims want to implement sharia law in their countries. Significant percentages believe that suicide bombing can be justified.

A few years ago, atheist Bill Maher was on the Charlie Rose PBS show trying to make the point about how dangerous Islam is. Charlie Rose responded with the typical comment that all religions have their dangerous fanatics. Bill Maher would have none of it. He argued that Islam is different.

He said: "Vast numbers of Christians do not believe that if you leave the Christian religion, you should be killed for it. Vast numbers of Christians do not treat women as second-class citizens. Vast numbers of Christians do not believe if you draw a picture of Jesus Christ you should be killed for it."[37]

He went on to quote from a Pew Research poll in Egypt that found that 80 percent believe stoning is

---

[37] Charlie Rose interview of Bill Maher, www.youtube.com/watch?v=qYC5pzbs9s8.

the appropriate punishment for adultery. Nearly all of them (88%) thought death was an appropriate punishment for leaving the Muslim religion.

He also talked about the outrage when ISIS is beheading people. But he then pointed to the number of people who had been recently beheaded in Saudi Arabia. Very few politicians or commentators protested these beheadings, often for non-violent crimes.

In Mecca, non-Muslims are not even allowed in the holy parts of the city. You don't have that in other religions, he explained, and they behead people there. Bill Maher asked, "If they were beheading people in Vatican City, which is the equivalent of Mecca, don't you think there would be a bigger outcry about it?" He called it the soft bigotry of low expectations with Muslim people.

William Kirkpatrick writes about "The Vast Majority Myth." He counters this idea with three propositions.[38] The first proposition is that "the vast majority of people are peaceful, until they're not." It is easy to find examples of people who were peaceful for a long time and then quickly turned violent. The vast majority of Hutus were behaving peacefully before the genocide in Rwanda in 1994. By years end, the Hutu managed to kill about 800,000 Tutsi using clubs and machetes. The vast majority of Europeans were behaving peacefully prior to World

---

[38] William Kirkpatrick, "The Vast Majority Myth," *Crisis Magazine*, 15 December 2015, www.crisismagazine.com/2015/the-vast-majority-myth.

War I. All of that changed in 1914 when the nations of the world went to war with each other.

The second proposition is the reality that the vast majority of people will go with the flow. The majority of the Hutu went with the flow. Many of the moderate Hutus who did not join in the killing were in turn killed by their fellow Hutus.

This proposition is especially true in Islam. Most Muslims (especially in this country) would just like to be left alone. They want to go about the business of earning a living and raising a family. But Kirkpatrick says that one of the built-in features of Islam is that you won't be left alone. It forces you to be good. And the way to be good is to conform to sharia law. This is especially true in a country that not only has sharia law but has also established a caliphate. By then all of the arguments for a militant form of Islam have been institutionalized.

The third proposition is that a majority of people in any society are women and children. Although some Hutu women took part in the slaughter of Tutsi, it is true that the vast majority did not. That is little comfort to those who were slaughtered. Most jihadists and suicide bombers are men, but there are some women and children that participate. While it is true that the vast majority aren't jihadists, that makes little difference in terms of the terrorist danger.

## Fighting Terrorism

Terrorism against democratic governments has often been successful because these governments are accustomed to dealing within a legal structure. Thus, they often find it difficult to deal with terrorists who routinely operate outside of the law. Yet deterrence is just as much a part of justice as proper enforcement of the laws.

Democratic governments that do not deter criminals inevitably spawn vigilantism as normally law-abiding citizens, who have lost confidence in the criminal justice system, take the law into their own hands. A similar backlash is beginning to emerge as a result of the inability of Western democracies to defend themselves against terrorists. Activists want to "bomb terrorists and terrorist nations back to the stone age." Pacifists want to retreat from a war on terror and find ways to appease those who threaten Western society.

Terrorists have also been successful due to media exposure. Terrorists thrive on media exposure, and news organizations (as well as website and blogs on the Internet) have been all too willing to give terrorists the publicity they desire. When kidnappings, hijackings, and bombings are given prominent media attention, governments start feeling pressure from their citizens to resolve the crisis. Often, they capitulate to the demands of terrorists and terrorist organizations. Encouraged by their latest success, terrorists usually try again. Appeasement, Churchill wisely noted, always whets the appetite, and recent successes have made terrorists hungry for more attacks.

Some news commentators have been unwilling to call terrorism what it is: wanton, criminal violence. Some news organizations refuse even to use the word "terrorist" in their broadcast. Others argue that "one man's terrorist is another man's freedom fighter." But this simply is not true. Terrorists are not concerned about human rights and human dignity. In fact, they end up destroying human rights in their alleged fight for human rights.

We should be asking the question, what is a terrorist? Is a terrorist a common criminal? If terrorists are only common criminals, then they are a problem for the host government. However, if terrorists are more like a foreign enemy of the government, then they should be treated as enemy combatants.

The answer to this question is no small issue. In recent decades, governments have oscillated in their answers to this question. How you answer the question will determine whether you bring terrorists to justice (treat them like criminals) or bring justice to terrorists (treat them like combatants). The Bible provides some guidance in Romans 13:2-4 where the Apostle Paul says:

> He who resists authority has opposed the ordinance of God; and they who have opposed will receive condemnation upon themselves. For rulers are not a cause of fear for good behavior, but for evil. Do you want to have no fear of authority? Do what is good and you will have praise from the same; for it is a minister of God to you for good. But if you do what is evil, be afraid; for it does not bear the sword for nothing; for it is a minister of God, an avenger who brings wrath upon the one who practices evil.

This passage of Scripture helps us make an important distinction in our analysis of terrorism. It shows that criminals are those who do evil and threaten the civil peace. Any outside threat to the existence of the state is not a criminal threat but an act of war, which is also to be dealt with by the government.

In other words, criminals threaten the state from within. Foreign armies threaten the state from outside. In the case of seeking domestic peace, Romans 13 outlines how governments will approve of good works, but that governments should bring fear to those that are wrongdoers.

Evildoers should live in fear of government. Terrorists do not live in fear of the governing authorities in the countries where they live. Some terrorist organizations live outside of the laws of their host government while others engage in terrorist activities with the approval of the host government.

Many Muslim terrorists do not even fear the "sword" of the governing authorities. Instead are often given sanctuary by such governments. Governments who give sanctuary and even give approval have often adopted the attitude that terrorists do them no harm so why should they move against the terrorist organizations? In fact, they are not seen as a threat because terrorist groups are acting out the host government's policies.

By definition, terrorist groups and their host nations are enemies of the government when they capture and kill innocent civilians for military and foreign policy purposes. When terrorists attack, the government should not view them as criminals but as foreign soldiers who attempt to threaten the very existence of that government.

The strategy and tactics of governments fighting terrorism have to change. In the same way that it took traditional armies some time to learn how to combat guerilla warfare, so it is taking time for Western governments to realize that the rules of warfare have also been revised in the case of terrorism.

## Declare War on Terrorists?

If Western governments say they are fighting a war on terrorism, shouldn't they formally declare war? This is a good question. Many have indeed called for a formal declaration of war rather than a more limited authorization for the use of power. A declaration of war would be an opportunity to thoroughly debate the issue as well as clearly define who the enemy in this struggle is.

The U.S. Constitution grants the following powers to Congress: "To define and punish piracies and felonies committed on the high seas, and offenses against the law of nations; To declare war, grant letters of marque and reprisal, and make rules concerning captures on land and water." Terrorist acts fall into at least two of the congressional provisions for dealing with attacks on the nation. They are (1) to punish offenses against the law of nations, and (2) to declare war.

In either case, there are strong Constitutional grounds for taking action against terrorists. The difficulty comes in clearly identifying the enemy and being willing to risk offending many nations in the Middle East whom we consider allies. Congress should identify the enemy and thus define that group as a military target. Once Congress does this, many other steps fall into place.

Military strategy should be deployed to hunt down small groups of well-armed and well-funded men who hide within the territory of a host country. Political strategy should be developed that will allow us to work within a host country. The government must make it clear how serious it takes a terrorist threat.

Diplomacy also can play a part. Using diplomatic channels, we should make two things very clear to the host country. First, they should catch and punish the terrorist groups themselves as civilian criminals. Or, second, they should extradite the enemy soldiers and give them up to an international court for trial.

If the host country fails to act on these two requests, we should make it clear that we see them in complicity with the terrorist groups. But failing to exercise their civil responsibility, they leave themselves open to the consequences of allowing hostile military forces within their borders.

## Terrorism and Just War

The Christian response to war has ranged from pacifism to activism. But most Christians hold to what has come to be known as the "just war tradition." This view developed over many centuries and drew from Greek and Roman sources until it was formalized into a structure by Augustine.

There are seven key principles in a just war. The first five apply to a nation "on the way to war" (*just ad bellum*) while the final two apply "in the midst of war" (*just in bello*). These are the seven principles in a just war:

1. Just cause. All aggression is condemned, only defensive war is legitimate.

2. Just intention. The only legitimate intention is to secure a just peace for all involved. Neither revenge nor conquest nor economic gain not ideological supremacy are justified.

3. Last resort. War may only be entered upon when all negotiations and compromise have been tried and failed.

4. Formal declaration. Since the use of military force is the prerogative of governments, not of private individuals, a state of war must be officially declared by the highest authorities.

5. Limited objectives. If the purpose is peace, then unconditional surrender or the destruction of a nation's economic or political institutions is an unwarranted objective.

5. Proportionate means. The weaponry and the force used should be limited to what is needed to repel the aggression and deter future attacks (in order to secure a just peace).

6. Noncombatant immunity. Since war is an official act of government, only those who are officially agents of a government may fight, and

individuals not actively contributing to the conflict should be immune from attack.

Although Christians may disagree about how to apply these principles in our current war on terrorism, they nevertheless provide a helpful framework for discussing this issue. For example, the principle of "proportionate means" leads to two conclusions:

• The military should not apply too severe a punishment. Calls for bombing cities of host countries in retaliation for terrorist actions should be rejected as inappropriate and unjust.

• The military should not apply too light a punishment. Host nations who harbor terrorists and refuse to punish or extradite terrorists should be pressured to do the right thing. Punishment could come in the form of economic embargoes, severing diplomatic relations, or even military actions. But the punishment should be proportional to the terrorist act.

Two types of objections often surface against the idea of a just war. First, there is a moral objection. Pacifists argue that it is never right to go to war and often cite biblical passages to bolster their argument. For example, Jesus said believers should turn the other cheek (Matt. 5:39). He also warned that "those who take up the sword shall perish by the sword" (Matt. 26:52).

The context of the statements is important. In the first instance, Jesus is speaking to individual believers in his Sermon on the Mount, admonishing believers not to engage in personal retaliation. In the second instance, He tells Peter to put down his sword because the gospel should not be advanced by the sword. But at the same time, Jesus actually encouraged his disciples to buy a sword (Luke 22:36) in order to protect themselves.

There is also a political objection. Critics say that the just war tradition applies to only to nations and not to terrorists. Even so, that would not invalidate military actions in Muslim countries that harbor terrorists.

But the criticism is incorrect. Christian thought about just war predates the concept of modern nation-states. So, the application of these principles can apply to governments or terrorist organizations. Moreover, the very first use of American military force in this country was against Barbary Pirates. President Thomas Jefferson actually declared war on the Muslim pirates who were from the Barbary Coast of Tripoli, Tunis, Morocco, and Algiers.

Before the Revolutionary War, American ships had been under the protection of England. Then the United States had to provide protection, but the Barbary pirates began to capture many of the ships. The United States (along with many European governments) began paying bribes to the Barbary States.

When Thomas Jefferson became president, the Pasha of Tripoli sent a note demanding the immediate payment of $225,000 a year plus additional amounts in future years. That was enough. Jefferson told the Pasha what he could do with the demand. The Pasha cut down the flagpole in Algiers and declared war on America. The other Barbarian States also declared war.

Congress and the president then responded by empowering American ships to seize all vessels and goods of the Pasha of Tripoli. Once the U.S. took action some of the other Barbary States backed down. The war with Tripoli lasted four more years. This included a battle in 1805 when the Marines raised the American flag not far from the shores of Tripoli. That became the famous line in the anthem of the Marine Corps.

# SECTION 3 Questions About Islam

We have many questions about Islam. Do Christians and Muslims worship the same God? How do Muslims view the Christian world? We also have many misconceptions about Islam. Is this religion a religion of peace? What about Islam and the Crusades?

# CHAPTER 7 – CHRISTIANS AND MUSLIMS

Christians and Muslims live in the same world, but they don't always understand each other. This chapter will look at some of the statements we often hear that aren't accurate and deserve further study. We will also look at some of the misconceptions Christians have about Muslims.

In particular, we will look at some of the politically correct phrases that sound nice but are not true. We hear that "Christians and Muslims worship the same God" and that "Islam is a religion of peace." If we are to understand Islam truly, we need to look carefully and work to understand the true nature of Christianity and Islam.

## Worship the Same God?

One politically correct phrase that is often repeated is that "Christians and Muslims worship the same God." It is understandable that people might say that. Both Islam and Christianity are monotheistic, even though a foundational difference is the Christian belief in the trinity.

The most foundational doctrine in Islam is monotheism. This doctrine is encapsulated in the creed: "There is no God but Allah, and Muhammad is the prophet of Allah." And not only is it a creed, it is a statement of faith that routinely heard from the lips of every faithful Muslim. It is the creed by which every Muslim is called to prayer five times a day.

Because of this strong emphasis on monotheism, Muslims reject the idea that God could be more than one person or that God could have a partner. The Qur'an teaches that Allah is one God and the same God for all people. Anyone who does not believe this is guilty of the sin of *shirk*. This is the quintessential sin in Islam. According to Islam, God cannot have a partner and cannot be joined together in the Godhead with other persons. Muslims, therefore, reject the Christian idea of the Trinity.

Muslims and Christians also differ in their understanding of the nature and character of God. The God of the Bible is knowable. Jesus came into the world that we might know God (John 17:3).

Islam teaches a very different view of God. Allah is distant, transcendent, and unknowable. He is separate from His creation. He is exalted and far removed from mankind. While we may know His will, we cannot know Him personally. In fact, there is very little written about the character of God. Allah is the creator and sustainer of the creation, but He is also unknowable. No person can ever personally know and have a relationship with Allah. Instead, humans are to be in total submission to the will of Allah.

Moreover, Allah does not personally enter into human history. Instead, he deals with the world through His word (the Qur'an), through His prophets (such as Muhammad), and through angels (such as Gabriel).

113

By contrast, Christianity teaches the fatherhood of God. Jesus taught in the Lord's Prayer that we may address God as "our Father in heaven." Christians can have a personal relationship with God through Christ and call God "Abba Father."

When a Muslim hears a Christian talk about God in such intimate terms, he or she might object. At an emotional level, it may be appealing even attractive. But at a conscious level, such talk also sounds jarring and even blasphemous.

A Christian and Muslim perspective on God's love is also very different. Christians begin with the belief that "God so loved the world" (John 3:16). By contrast, Muslims grow up hearing about all the people Allah does not love. Sura 2:190 says, "For Allah loves not transgressors." Sura 3:32 says, "Allah loves not the unbelievers." Finally, we see that Sura 3:57 says, "For Allah loves not the evildoers."

## Muslim View of Jesus as the Son of God

As we have mentioned, the Qur'an refers to Jesus as "the Messiah" or "the Christ" (Sura 4:157) and also calls him "the word of God" (Sura 3:45). But Muslims reject the idea that God could have a Son.

Sura 19:35 says, "It is not befitting Allah that He should beget a son. Glory to Him! When He determines a matter, He only says to it, 'Be,' and it is." Muhammad believed that begetting a son would essentially make Allah a sexual animal, so he rejected the idea that God could have a Son. He believed that it would be beneath God's dignity to have sexual relations. Sura 2:116 says, "They say, 'Allah hath begotten a son': Glory be to Him—Nay, to Him belongs all that is in the heavens and on earth: everything renders worship to Him."

Some Muslim commentators have said that the idea that God could have a Son in a relic of paganism. They even believe that it is blasphemous to say that, "Allah begets sons like a man or animal."[39]

This, however, is not what Christianity teaches. The Bible does not say that God had sex and begat a Son. While that might have been the belief expressed in the Greek myths where gods has sex with each other and with humans, it is not the teaching of Christianity.

Jesus Christ is called the Son of God. God is heard from heaven declaring, "This is My beloved Son in whom I am well pleased" (Matt. 17:5). Also, believers are called children of God: "See how great a love the Father has bestowed on us, that we would be called children of God" (1 John 3:1).

Let's compare Jesus and Muhammad. Muslims believe that Muhammad is the final prophet from Allah. He is referred to as the "seal of the prophets" (Sura 33:40). But while he is revered as the greatest of the prophets, most do not teach that he was sinless. The Qur'an does not make the claim that he was sinless, and there are passages that teach that Muhammad was a man like us (Sura 18:110) and that

---

[39] Abdullah Yusuf Ali, *The Holy Qur'an: Text, Translation, and Commentary* (Brentwood, MD: Amana Corporation, 1989), 49.

Allah told Muhammad that he must repent of his sins (Sura 40:55).

By contrast, Jesus claimed to be God and claimed to have the powers and authority that only God could possess. The New Testament provides eyewitness accounts or records of eyewitness accounts of the claims that Jesus made and the miracles he performed. Moreover, the New Testament teaches that Jesus Christ lived a perfect and sinless life (2 Cor. 5:21).

Muhammad also taught that Muslims are to fight in the cause of Allah (Sura 4:76) and fight against the unbelievers (Sura 9:123). By contrast, Jesus taught that Christians are to love their enemies (Matt. 5:44) and turn the other cheek (Matt. 5:39).

The life of Muhammad is different from many of the other founders of religion. Moreover, the life of Muhammad and the life of Jesus Christ are very different.

## Muslim View of The Trinity

Islam was founded in order to return all religions to a true worship of the one true God. Muslims, therefore, reject any religion that does not rest upon the belief in monotheism. The doctrine of the trinity sounds to Muslims as a corruption of the belief in monotheism. In fact, it sounds like a compromise of the unity and oneness of God.

Two key verses in the Qur'an refer to the doctrine of the trinity. Sura 4:171 says, "O people of the book! Commit no excesses in your religions: nor say of Allah aught but the truth. Christ Jesus, the son of Mary, was (no more than) a messenger of Allah, and His World, which He bestowed on Mary." The verse continues, "Say not 'Trinity': desist: it will be better for you; for Allah is One God: glory be to Him."

Another passage is Sura 5:73: "They do blaspheme who say: Allah is one of three in a Trinity' for there is no God except One God. If they desist not from their word (of blasphemy), verily, a grievous penalty will befall the blasphemers among them."

Later in that chapter (Sura 5:116-117) there is a conversation that supposedly takes place between Jesus and God on judgment day: "And behold! Allah will say: 'O Jesus the son of Mary! Didst thou say unto men, "Worship me and my mother as gods in derogation of Allah?" He will say, 'Glory to Thee! Never could I say what I had no right (to say). Had I said such a thing, Thou wouldst indeed have known it. Thou knowest what is in my heart, though I know not what is in Thine . . . . Never said I to them aught except what Thou didst command me to say, to wit, "Worship Allah – my Lord and your Lord."

The Bible teaches that God has revealed Himself in three distinct persons: the Father, the Son and the Holy Spirit. These three persons make up the one true God. These three persons are of the same substance, equal in power and glory.

The Bible clearly states that there is only one God. Deuteronomy 6:4 states, "Hear O Israel, the Lord is our God, the Lord is one." Isaiah 44:6 states, "I am the first and I am the last, and there is no God besides me." Clearly, these verses reveal that there is only one God. Yet, there are three separate persons in the Bible who are called God and have the characteristics only God can have.

Throughout scripture, the Father is called God. The Son is also called God (John 20:28, Matthew 1:23, Titus 2:13). The Son is worshipped, has authority over areas only God has authority over. The Son shares in the attributes only God can have. The Holy Spirit is also called God (Matthew 28:19, Acts 5:3-4, Romans 8). All three are equal in nature yet there is an economy among the persons of the Trinity.

We also can see that the disciples referred to Jesus as God. In John 20:28 Thomas, after seeing the resurrected Lord, proclaims to Jesus, "My Lord and My God." We see, therefore, that Thomas calls Jesus *God*. And when John wrote his gospel, he begins by saying, "In the beginning was the Word, and the Word was with God, and the Word was God" (John 1:1).

## A Religion of Peace?

One politically correct phrase that is often repeated is that "Islam is a religion of peace." Certainly, most the Muslims we meet want to live in peace and make good citizens. But is it true that all of Islam has been peaceful? To answer that question, it is important to return to our discussion of the word "jihad."

Although some Muslims understand jihad to be merely intellectual and philosophical, the usual translation of jihad involves a holy war. That has been the traditional interpretation since the time of Muhammad.

Jihad was to be waged on the battlefield. Sura 47:4 says, "When you meet the unbelievers in the battlefield, strike off their heads and, when you have laid them low, bind your captives firmly." Sura 9:5 says, "Fight and slay the pagans wherever you find them, and seize them, beleager them, and lie in wait for them in every stratagem."

Consider some of these other passages concerning jihad. Faithful Muslims wage jihad against unbelievers: "Fight in the cause of Allah those who fight you . . . . and slay them wherever you catch them . . . . and fight them on until there is no more tumult or oppression, and there prevail justice and faith in Allah" (Sura 2:190-193).

Here are two other similar passages that talk about fighting unbelievers. "Soon shall We cast terror into the hearts of the unbelievers, for that they joined companions with Allah, for what He had no authority: their abode will be the Fire: And evil is the home of the wrong-doers" (Sura 3:151). Also, "O ye who believe! Fight the unbelievers who gird your about, and let them find firmness in you; and know that Allah is with those who fear Him" (Sura 9:123).

Muslims are also to wage jihad not only against unbelievers but against those who have strayed from the faith:

• Sura 4:89 – "They but wish that ye should reject Faith, as they do, and thus be on the same footing (as they): so take not friends from their ranks until they flee in the way of Allah. . . . But if they turn renegades, seize them and slay them wherever ye find them."

• Sura 9:73 – "Prophet, make war on the unbelievers and the hypocrites and deal rigorously with them. Hell shall be their home: and evil fate."

The Qur'an also teaches that engaging in jihad is good for a Muslim: "Fighting is prescribed upon you, and ye dislike it. But it is possible that ye dislike a thing which is good for you, and that ye love a thing which is bad for you. But Allah knoweth and ye know not" (Sura 2:216). The Qur'an (4:95) also exalts "those who strive and fight in the cause of Allah with their goods and persons" above "those who sit and receive no hurt."

Another way to understand the term "jihad" is to look at the historical context. After Muhammad's success in the Battle of Badr, he set forth various principles of warfare. For example, according to Sura 9:29, jihad is a religious duty. Muhammad taught (in Sura 3:157-158, 195; 9:111) that martyrdom in jihad is the highest good and guarantees salvation. Sura 9:5 says that Muslims engaged in jihad should not show tolerance toward unbelievers. And acts of terrorism are justified in Sura 8:2.

Muhammad also promised that they would be victorious in jihad even when they were outnumbered. "Exhort the believers to fight. If there be of you twenty steadfast they shall overcome two hundred, and if there be of you a hundred (steadfast) they shall overcome a thousand of those who disbelieve, because they (the disbelievers) are a folk without intelligence" (Sura 8:65).

Some of the violence commanded in the Qur'an is actually quite gruesome:

• Sura 5:33 – "The punishment of those who wage war against Allah and His Messenger, and strive with might and main for mischief through the land is: execution, or crucifixion, or the cutting off of hands and feet from opposite sides, or exile from the land: that is their disgrace in this world, and a punishment is theirs in the hereafter."

• Sura 8:12-13 – "Smite ye above their necks and smite all their fingertips off them. This because they contend against Allah and His Messenger, Allah is strict in punishment."

## The Qur'an and Murder

Muslims often will quote a passage in the Qur'an to show that it prohibits murder. It says, "Whosoever kills a human being for other than manslaughter or corruption in the earth, it shall be as if he had killed all mankind, and whoever saves the life of one, it shall be as if he had saved the life of all mankind" (Sura 5:32).

This passage is not really a prohibition against murder, for two reasons. First, the passage is addressed to the "Children of Israel" in a particular historical context. It is not addressed to Muslims. Actually, it was a warning to the Jews not to engage in warfare against Muhammad.

Second, it has an important proviso: if there is corruption in the earth. This is sometimes translated as "making mischief in the land." While this would certainly include making war against the Muslims, it could also include resisting the Muslim advance into the land. The penalty for making mischief in the land was the following: "execution, or crucifixion, or the cutting off of hands and feet from opposite sides, or exile from the land."

## Violence in the Bible and the Qur'an

Whenever verses of the sword from the Qur'an are quoted, usually someone will quickly point out that the Old Testament calls for violence. But are these two books morally equivalent? Let's look at some of these passages and see.

The Qur'an calls for jihad against the unbelievers (or infidels). Sura 9:5 says, "Fight and slay the pagans wherever you find them, and seize them, beleager them, and lie in wait for them in every stratagem."

Sura 9:29 says, "Fight those who believe not in Allah nor the Last Day, nor hold that forbidden which hath been forbidden by Allah and His Prophet, nor acknowledge the religion of Truth, (even if they are) of the People of the Book, until they pay the *jizyah* [per capita tax imposed on non-Muslim adult males] with willing submission, and feel themselves subdued."

Sura 47:4-7 says, "When you meet unbelievers, smite their necks, then, when you have made wide slaughter among them, tie fast the bonds; then set them free, either by grace or ransom, till the war lays down its loads...And those who are slain in the way of God, He will not send their works astray. He will guide them, and dispose their minds aright, and He will admit them to Paradise, that He has made known to them."

In the Old Testament, there sometimes was a call for military action against specific groups. Deuteronomy 7:1-2 says, "When the Lord your God brings you into the land where you are entering to possess it, and clears away many nations before you, the Hittites and the Girgashites and the Amorites and the Canaanites and the Perizzites and the Hivites and the Jebusites, seven nations greater and stronger than you, and when the Lord your God delivers them before you and you defeat them, then you shall utterly destroy them. You shall make no covenant with them and show no favor to them."

1 Samuel 15:2-3 says, "Thus says the Lord of hosts, I will punish Amalek for what he did to Israel, how he set himself against him on the way while he was coming up from Egypt. Now go and strike Amalek and utterly destroy all that he has, and do not spare him; but put to death both man and woman, child and infant, ox and sheep, camel and donkey."

While there are some similarities, notice the difference. In the Old Testament, there was a *direct* and *specific* command to fight against a particular group of people. These passages do not apply to anyone who is not a Hittite, Girgashite, Amorite, Canaanite, Perizzite, Hivite, Jebusite, or Amalekite. These commands given during the Old Testament theocracy apply only to those people at that time.

The passages are also quite specific. In 1 Samuel 15, the military action is to be taken only against the Amalekites. Notice that in verse 6 that Saul says to the Kenites, "Go, depart, go down from among the Amalekites so that I do not destroy you with them." So specific is the command that he sends the Kenites away so they might not be hurt by any collateral damage.

While the passages in the Old Testament apply specifically to a particular group of people, the passages in the Qur'an apply to all unbelievers at all times. Notice that there is no time limit on these universally binding commands to all Muslims at all times.

No Christian leader is calling for a Holy War against infidels. But many Muslim leaders cite the Qur'an for that very action. Osama bin Laden, for example, quoted many of these verses of the sword just cited within his various *fatwas*.

Contrast this with the New Testament which calls for believers to love their enemies (Matt. 5:44) and turn the other cheek (Matt. 5:39). Christians are called to love (not hate) their enemies, to pray for them, and to not respond with a violent jihad with those with whom they disagree.

## Muslim View of the Christian World

The average Muslim in other parts of the world often has a great misunderstanding of Western Christianity. Often their own experience with the U.S. and the rest of the world comes from our cultural export: the media. What they know about us is in our movies, music, and television programs. Thus, they perceive America and the rest of the Western world as full of sex and violence. Since they believe America is a Christian nation, they assume that everything that comes from our country (and the rest of the West) illustrates Christian attitudes and behavior. So they often equate Christianity with promiscuous sex, rampant drug use, violence and social strife.

When you talk with a Muslim, you should clarify that what they frequently see of the West does not necessarily align with biblical Christianity. Christians are equally concerned about the sex, pornography, violence, and profanity in the media and even in daily life. Help him or her to understand your moral concerns about these very same issues.

## Why It Is Hard for Muslims to Become Christians

One of the reasons it is hard for Muslims to come to Christ was just mentioned. They are often repulsed by the Western world and equate Western decadence with Christianity. They reason that if that is what Christian is, then they don't want any part of it. It is important to clear up many of the misconceptions Muslims may have about Christianity.

Another reason it is hard for Muslims to become Christian is cultural. It has been said the Islam is 10 percent theological and 90 percent cultural. To reject Islam is to reject one's family and culture. The average Muslim desires (as we all do) to be part of a larger cultural group in order to feel secure and be affirmed.

125

The Muslim culture also reinforces these beliefs and provides a safe haven in a world of threats and confusion. When a Muslim hears the claims of Christ, he or she may be drawn to the truth but refuse to make a commitment because of the heavy cost of that commitment. Leaving Islam can mean the loss of family, the loss of community, even the loss of life.

A Muslim needs to be able to find a safe Christian community to join after their conversion. Unfortunately, in many parts of the world, such communities do not exist.

## Witnessing to Muslims about Jesus

Muslims accept that the Qur'an teaches them all they need to know about Jesus Christ. They accept that He is the Messiah and the Christ. And they honor him as one of the greatest prophets. So they feel they already believe everything that needs to be believed about Him. So they feel uncomfortable when Christians tell them that they need to believe in Jesus Christ. After all, they already believe in Him and already honor Him.

While Muslims may know that the Qur'an gives titles to Jesus such as "Messiah" and the "Word of God," they have no context for understanding what those titles mean. You should explain what these titles meant in the Old Testament and how they found their fulfillment in the person of Jesus Christ.

Show them from the Qur'an what it really says about Jesus. For example, Sura 3:42-55 teaches that: (1) Mary was chosen by God, (2) Jesus was born of a virgin, (3) Jesus is the Messiah, (4) Jesus has power

126

over death, and (5) Jesus knows the way to heaven. These verses ascribe power and position to Jesus that Muhammad did not ascribe to himself.

Many Muslims are not aware that the following assertions appear in the Qur'an:

• If you are in doubt about the truth, ask those who read the Scripture that came before you (Sura 10:94).

• To be a proper Muslim, one must read the Old and New Testament, known as the Before Books (Sura 4:136).

• Those who observe the teaching of the Torah and the Gospels will go to heaven Koran (Sura 5:65-66).

• Mohammed states he is not the greatest prophet, he does not know what will happen to his followers (after death) and he is only a Warner (Sura 46:9).

These passages are great conversation-starters about the Bible, Jesus, and salvation. They give Muslims permission to read the Bible and to learn spiritual truth from Christians.

Finally, make sure you talk about the love of God. As we have mentioned, Muslims believe that Allah is distant and unknowable. Christianity offers them the possibility of knowing God personally. This is attractive to Muslims.

A seminary conducted a survey of six hundred former Muslims who had become Christians. One most significant factors involved in the conversions of these former Muslims was the emphasis on the love of God and the intimacy that believers can have with God as their heavenly Father.[40] This was an important factor in drawing these former Muslims to Christ, so make sure you talk about the love of God.

---

[40] R.C. Sproul and Abdul Saleeb, *The Dark Side of Islam* (Wheaton, IL: Crossway Books, 2003), 33

# CHAPTER 8 – ISLAM AND THE CRUSADES

The Crusades were a series of military campaigns first declared by the Pope in an effort to reclaim the Holy Land from the Muslims. The Crusaders left jobs and family to take up arms and fight in the cause for Christendom. The word Crusade is taken from the Latin word *crux* or cross.

There were nine crusades. Although most of them were sanctioned by the Pope, there were other military campaigns later that are sometimes also called crusades. These continued into the sixteenth century. The Crusades had a political, economic, and social impact not only on those societies but even to this day.

## Reason for the Crusades

As we have previously discussed, Islam spread rapidly through the Middle East and even into Europe in the hundred years after the death of Muhammad. This rapid expansion included Muslims conquering territories that previously had been within the control of Christians. For example, the cities of Antioch, Alexandria, and Carthage had been the centers of Christian thought. They all fell to Muslim armies engaged in jihad and quickly conquering what had been Christian lands.

Jerusalem fell in 638, and this began centuries of persecution of Christians. Early in the eighth century, sixty Christian pilgrims from Amorium were crucified. During that same period, the Muslim governor of Caesarea rounded up a group of pilgrims from Iconium and had them executed as spies. By the end of that century, the Muslim caliph in Jerusalem required that all Christians and Jews have their hands stamped with a distinctive symbol. By the ninth century, large numbers of Christians fled to Constantinople and other Christian cities.

A key date in the history of the Crusades was 1095. In that year, the Byzantine Emperor Alexius I requested help from Pope Urban. The Turks had already conquered much of the Byzantine Empire, and Alexius needed mercenaries to help him resist Muslim advances into their territory. In fact, the city of Constantinople (perhaps the greatest Christian city in the world at that time) was threatened. Pope Urban at the Council of Clermont called upon Christians in Europe to respond to this plea.

While he knew that there was a need for the Christians to fight the Turks, he also knew that calling for that military action to save Eastern Christendom alone would not motivate many. So in order to motivate the faithful, he set forth a second goal: to free Jerusalem and the birthplace of Christ from Muslim rule.

This was not an arbitrary goal the Pope added to the list. In the years leading up to 1095, the Fatimid caliph, Abu 'Ali al-Hakim had destroyed thirty thousand churches including the Church of the Holy Sepulchre in Jerusalem. Many Christians during that time considered al-Hakim to be the Antichrist.

The Pope also added something else to the call for military action: the possibility of the remission of sins. During the medieval period, the idea of a pilgrim's vow was prominent. The crusaders vowed to reach the Holy Sepulcher in Jerusalem in return for the Pope's pardon for sins they had committed.

Pope Urban probably reasoned that a crusade would serve to reunite Christendom and perhaps even bring the East under his control. But once the Pope launched the first crusade, he had virtually no control over it. Those involved in the crusade made their decisions about tactics and strategy apart from the Pope.

### Brief History of the Crusades

Although there were many military campaigns called crusades, when we refer to "the Crusades" we are talking about the nine military campaigns that took place between 1095 and 1272. These were launched from Western Europe against the Muslims in the Middle East.

1. *The First Crusade (1095-1099)* – this began when the Byzantine emperor Alexius asked for Pope Urban to send mercenaries to join a war against the Turks. It was the most successful crusade. The Crusaders defeated the Turks and were also able to take Jerusalem. They established several states including the Kingdom of Jerusalem.

2. *The Second Crusade* (1145-1149) – this was an unsuccessful attempt to recapture a Crusader state (Edessa). And it endangered the other Crusader states because of an unwise attack on Damascus.

3. *The Third Crusade* (1189-1192) – this was also known as the King's Crusade and was called by Pope Gregory in the wake of Saladin's capture of Jerusalem in 1187. Many famous people participated in this Crusade, including King Richard the Lionhearted of England and King Phillip of France.

4. *The Fourth Crusade* (1201-1204) – this was initiated by Pope Innocent but was diverted to Constantinople by someone seeking the Byzantine throne. After much confusion and misunderstanding, the Crusaders sacked the city in 1204. This shocked the Christian world and further weakened the Byzantine Empire.

5. *The Fifth Crusade* (1217-1221) – this Crusade focused on Egypt with the assumption that by breaking Egyptian power, they could recapture Jerusalem. While they did capture Damietta, they foolishly attacked Cairo and failed.

6. *The Sixth Crusade* (1228-1229) – was a continuation of the Fifth Crusade. It came about because Emperor Frederick had repeatedly vowed a crusade, but never kept his word. The Pope excommunicated him in 1228. He set sail to the Holy Land and was able to negotiate a truce that allowed Christians to live in Jerusalem. But since the city was defenseless, the Muslims were able to take the city in 1244. Christians were killed, and many churches burned, including the Church of the Holy Sepulcher.

7. *The Seventh Crusade* (1248-1254) – was the best-equipped Crusade led by Louis IX of France against Egypt from 1248 to 1254. In the midst of one

battle, he was captured and later ransomed and returned to Europe.

8. *The Eighth Crusade* (1270) – this was also organized by Louis IX who came to the aid of the Crusader states in Syria. The Crusade was diverted to Tunis, where Louis died.

9. *The Ninth Crusade* (1271-1272) – was organized by the future Edward I of England who had accompanied Louis IX on the Eighth Crusade. Little was accomplished, and Edward retired the following year after a truce.

## Atrocities in the Crusades

Anyone who wants to criticize Christianity will most likely bring up the crusades and talk about the atrocities committed by Crusaders. It is certainly true that the Crusaders slaughtered Jews and Muslims in the sacking of Jerusalem. It is also true that the Crusaders even fought among themselves.

However, the true story of the Crusades is more complex than the typical criticism of Christianity. Both Muslims and Christians committed atrocities and brought about considerable carnage.

Muslims were also merciless and were barbaric in their treatment of Christians and Jews. Consider what the Turks did with the German and French prisoners captured in the First Crusade (prior to the sacking of Jerusalem). If they renounced Christ and converted to Islam, they were sent to the East. If they did not, they were slaughtered.

The great Muslim leader Saladin was not as merciful as he has been portrayed in the movies. For example, after defeating a large Latin army in 1187, he ordered the mass execution of all Hospitallers and Templars left alive. He personally beheaded the nobleman Reynald of Chatillon.

Saladin is best known for re-conquering Jerusalem, and much is made of his willingness to allow the Christians in Jerusalem who fought against him to live. But the true story is that he had originally planned to massacre all of the Christians in Jerusalem after taking it back from the Crusaders. However, when the commander of the Jerusalem threatened to destroy the city and kill all of the Muslims inside the walls, Saladin changed his plan. He allowed them to buy their freedom. If they could not do so, they were sold into slavery.

## Hollywood Films About the Crusades

There have been a number of films made about the Crusades, but the most expensive film (over $150 million) ever made about the Crusades is *Kingdom of Heaven*. It featured an all-star cast (Orlando Bloom, Jeremy Irons, Liam Neesom) and an extensive publicity budget. So how accurate is it?

The script was full of politically correct clichés and does a disservice to those trying to understand this period of history. The film invents a tolerance group known as the "Brotherhood of Muslims, Jews, and Christians." No such group existed. It also makes it seem as if this brotherhood of tolerance would have held together if certain Christian extremists didn't cause such problems.

Professor Jonathan Riley-Smith is a professor at Cambridge University and the author of *A Short History of the Crusades*. He called the film "rubbish" and said it was "not historically accurate at all." He complained that it "depicts the Muslims as sophisticated and civilized, and the Crusaders are all brutes and barbarians. It has nothing to do with reality."[41]

Professor Jonathan Phillips is a lecturer at London University and the author of *The Fourth Crusade and the Sack of Constantinople*. He said the film relied on an outdated portrayal of the Crusades and the Knights Templar. He says it is bad history: "The Templars as 'baddies' is only sustainable from the Muslim perspective, and 'baddies' is the wrong way to show it anyway. They are the biggest threat to the Muslims and many ends up being killed because of their sworn vocation is to defend the Holy Land."[42]

---

[41] Charlotte Edwardes, "Ridley Scott's new Crusades film panders to Osama bin Laden," *London Telegraph*, 18 Jan. 2004, http://www.telegraph.co.uk/news/main.jhtml?xml=/news/2004/01/18/wcrus18.xml&sSheet=/news/2004/01/18/ixworld.html.

[42] Ibid.

# Bibliography

Anderson, Kerby. *A Biblical Point of View on Islam*. Eugene, OR: Harvest House, 2008

Caner, Ergun and Emir Caner, *Unveiling Islam*. Grand Rapids, MI: Kregel, 2002.

Darwish, Nonie, *Now They Call Me Infidel*. NY: Sentinel, 2006.

Denison, Jim. *Radical Islam: What You Need to Know*. Elevation Press: 2011.

Dyer, Charles. *The ISIS Crisis*. Chicago, Moody, 2015.

Demy, Timothy and Gary Stewart, *In the Name of God: Understanding the Mindset of Terorrism*. Eugene, OR: Harvest House, 2002.

Douglass-Williams, Christine. *The Challenge of Modernizing Islam* (NY: Encounter, 2017).

Gabriel, Brigette. *Because They Hate*. NY: St. Martin's Press, 2006.

Geisler, Norman. *Answering Islam: The Crescent in Light of the Cross*. Grand Rapids, MI: Baker, 2002.

Huntington, Samuel. *The Clash of Civilizations*. NY; Simon and Schuster, 1996.

Lindsey, Hal. *The Everlasting Hatred: The Roots of Jihad*. Washington: WND Books, 2011.

Moore, Johnnie; *Defying Isis*. Nashville: Thomas Nelson, 2015.

Morey, Robert. *The Islamic Invasion*. Eugene, OR: Harvest House, 1992.

Qureshi, Nabeel. *Seeking Allah, Finding Jesus*. Grand Rapids, MI: Zondervan, 2016.

Rassamni, Jerry. *From Jihad to Jesus*. Chattanooga, TN: Living Ink Books, 2006.

Rosenberg, Joel. *Inside the Revolution*. Carol Stream, IL: Tyndal House, 2009.

Sekulow, Jay, et. al. *Rise of Isis*. NY: Howard, 2014.

Spencer, Robert *The Politically Incorrect Guide to Islam (And the Crusades)*. Washington: Regenery, 2005.

Spencer, Robert. *The Truth About Muhammad*. Washington, Regnery, 2006.

Sproul, R.C. and Abdul Saleeb, *The Dark Side of Islam*. Wheaton, IL: Crossway, 2003.

Youssef, Michael. *Jesus, Jihad and Peace*. Nashville, TN: Worthy, 2015.

www.ingramcontent.com/pod-product-compliance
Lightning Source LLC
LaVergne TN
LVHW051349080426
835509LV00020BA/3359